Hindu Mythology

A Captivating Guide to Hindu Myths, Hindu Gods, and Hindu Goddesses

© Copyright 2018

All rights Reserved. No part of this book may be reproduced in any form without permission in writing from the author. Reviewers may quote brief passages in reviews.

Disclaimer: No part of this publication may be reproduced or transmitted in any form or by any means, mechanical or electronic, including photocopying or recording, or by any information storage and retrieval system, or transmitted by email without permission in writing from the publisher.

While all attempts have been made to verify the information provided in this publication, neither the author nor the publisher assumes any responsibility for errors, omissions or contrary interpretations of the subject matter herein.

This book is for entertainment purposes only. The views expressed are those of the author alone, and should not be taken as expert instruction or commands. The reader is responsible for his or her own actions.

Adherence to all applicable laws and regulations, including international, federal, state and local laws governing professional licensing, business practices, advertising and all other aspects of doing business in the US, Canada, UK or any other jurisdiction is the sole responsibility of the purchaser or reader.

Neither the author nor the publisher assumes any responsibility or liability whatsoever on the behalf of the purchaser or reader of these materials. Any perceived slight of any individual or organization is purely unintentional.

Free Bonus from Captivating History (Available for a Limited time)

Hi History Lovers!

Now you have a chance to join our exclusive history list so you can get your first history ebook for free as well as discounts and a potential to get more history books for free! Simply visit the link below to join.

Captivatinghistory.com/ebook

Also, make sure to follow us on:

Twitter: @Captivhistory

Facebook: Captivating History:@captivatinghistory

Contents

INTRODUCTION: UNDERSTANDING HINDU MYTHOLOGY 1
   MISTS OF HISTORY 1
   MODERN HINDUISM: FOUR BRANCHES 2
   HOLY TEXTS: SHRUTI AND SMRTI 3
   PHILOSOPHY 3
   MYTHS AND LEGENDS 3

CHAPTER 1: LORD BRAHMA, LORD VISHNU, AND THE BEGINNING OF THE WORLD 5

CHAPTER 2: THE BIRTH OF LORD SHIVA 7

CHAPTER 3: SARASWATI & BRAHMA'S FIFTH HEAD 10

CHAPTER 4: SHIVA TESTS PARVATI 12

CHAPTER 5: SHIVA SNARES A WHALE 15

CHAPTER 6: GANESHA LOSES HIS HEAD 19

CHAPTER 7: GANESHA SPILLS A RIVER 22

CHAPTER 8: KUBERA'S PRIDE 24

CHAPTER 9: GANESHA INJURES A GODDESS 27

CHAPTER 10: GANESHA WINS A RACE 29

CHAPTER 11: SHIVA SKIPS SUCCESS 31

CHAPTER 12: RAVANA'S TEN HEADS 33

CHAPTER 13: THE BIRTH OF RAMA 36

CHAPTER 14: URMILA'S SLUMBER 39

CHAPTER 15: DEER OF DECEPTION 42

CHAPTER 16: HANUMAN'S TORCH 45

CHAPTER 17: SUVANNAMACHHA STEALS A BRIDGE 48

CHAPTER 18: HANUMAN MOVES A MOUNTAIN 51

CHAPTER 19: THE FINAL BATTLE	54
CHAPTER 20: SITA'S PURITY	57
CHAPTER 21: KRISHNA STEALS BUTTER	60
CHAPTER 22: KRISHNA TRADES FOR JEWELS	63
CHAPTER 23: KRISHNA SWALLOWS THE FLAMES	65
CHAPTER 24: AGNI SPREADS A CURSE	67
CHAPTER 25: VAYU HUMBLES THE SILK COTTON TREE	70
CHAPTER 26: SAVITRI CHOOSES A HUSBAND	73
CHAPTER 27: SAVITRI'S FIDELITY	76
CHAPTER 28: CHITRAGUPTA TAKES NOTES	79
CHAPTER 29: ASHES TO ASHES	82
BIBLIOGRAPHY	102
FREE BONUS FROM CAPTIVATING HISTORY (AVAILABLE FOR A LIMITED TIME)	103

Introduction: Understanding Hindu Mythology

At first glance, Hindu myth may seem confusing. Gods and men lose their heads (literally), appear by different names, and occasionally form rivers from watering pots—and that's just in one corner of the Puranas.

Keep in mind people have spent generations writing about and discussing these stories and beliefs; it's natural for your brain to hurt a little bit as you sort it all out. Just imagine you're at your boyfriend or girlfriend's family reunion trying to figure out how everyone's related. (Or not related, in some cases. Some people really do just show up for the pizza.)

Mists of History

The birth of Hinduism occurred, according to archeologists and anthropologists, in the Indus valley when two Indo-European tribes mingled their respective belief systems. The two tribes, the Aryans, and the Dravidians, combined their practices and pantheons, from which combination (over the course of several thousand years) emerged the Trimurti, the holy trinity of Hindu Gods. The Trimurti includes Brahma, the creator; Vishnu, the protector of the world; and Shiva, the maintainer, and destroyer. Other familiar gods from the

Aryan culture (the nomads) include Indra, Soma, Agni, and Varuna. For the most part, these gods are still sought after and celebrated in the Hindu traditions today.

Modern Hinduism: Four Branches

The stories in Hindu myth stem from traditions within Hinduism, drawing on stories from ancient texts, like the Ramayana and the Mahabharata. The major traditions include Vaishnavism, Shaivism, Shaktism, and Smarta. Subtraditions include Nath, Lingayatism, Atimarga, Sauraism, and others.

Though the four major traditions might share ceremonies or even beliefs, Vaishnavism, Shaivism, Shaktism, and Smarta each propound their own practices and philosophies.

Vaishnavism or *Vishnuisim* believes Vishnu is the supreme manifestation of God. Other gods and demigods—like Rama and Krishna—are, in fact, visualizations of Vishnu and his greatness. The followers of this sect, called Vaishnavas, are non-ascetic, meaning they're not interested in extremely simple lifestyles. i.e., sackcloth and ashes (in the Christian tradition) or other forms of self-denial for the sake of enlightenment.

Shaivism, considered the largest contingent within the Hindu tradition, believes Shiva is the supreme manifestation of God. Shaivites or Saivites spread to Southeast Asia, building temples and spreading their taste for yoga and the ascetic life with them. In some areas, Shaivism and Buddhism evolved together; some Shaivist temples feature Buddhist symbols and carvings.

Shaktism, closely related to Shaivism, believes "The Goddess" is the supreme manifestation of God. "The Goddess" is the divine feminine, worshipped in the form of Devi or Shakti. Devi is a partner with Shiva.

Smarta believes in Panchatayana puja, or equal worship for five main gods and goddesses: Shiva, Vishnu, Surya, Devi, and Ganesha.

If you want to keep the different contingents straight, remember:

Vaishnaivism=Vishnu
Shaivism=Shiva
Shaktism "shakes it up" with Shakti. Belief in the divine feminine.
Smarta=5 letters in "smart" for 5 different gods

Holy Texts: Shruti and Smrti

The stories from Hindu myth originate from two different books of scripture—the shruti and smrti.

Shruti, meaning "that which is heard" forms the backbone of Hindu philosophy. The Vedas, the Brahmanas, and the Upanishad fall into this category. The Shruti are considered authorless and ageless.

Smrti, meaning "that which is remembered" includes the Puranas and the Epics, like the Ramayana and Mahabharata. The Smrti are attributed to an author. The Bhagavad Gita is part of the Mahabharata.

Philosophy

The Hindu philosophical traditions include the Sankhya, Yoga, Nyaya, Vaisheshika, Mimamsa, and Vedanta. These—the Astika, or orthodox—accept the Vedas as authoritative. The Nastika—the unorthodox—reject the Vedas and include Buddhism, Jainism, Carvaka, and Ajivika.

The Astika philosophies are traced through the Vedas and other Hindu scriptures, popping up alongside mythological facts and figures. They shape the perspective in the stories and make up the ontological bones.

Myths and Legends

Why does any of this background matter?

The myths you're about to read are steeped in these foundations. These stories—Ravana the rakshasa and his ten heads, Lord Ganesha and his mouse mount, the protection of Krishna—are really about the people who tell them and the meaning they try to make of them. A basic understanding of the roots of Hinduism can help you to find the golden threads among an intricate tapestry of heritage and belief. The symbols of these myths—lotus flowers, multiple heads or arms, tapasyas—richly represent thousands of years of perspective and worship.

Keep in mind that because different versions of Hinduism inspire different people, many different versions of the stories float through the jungle and over the stones of temples and traditions. The stories in this volume are my version, though I've stuck as closely to the original myths and legends as imagination allows. At the end of this book, you'll find a short bibliography for further research and reading.

Namaste.

Chapter 1: Lord Brahma, Lord Vishnu, and the Beginning of the World

In the beginning, there was only nothingness and the Brahman. (Not to be confused with Brahma—he came later.) The Brahman—formless and beyond description—drew out the nothingness and created beings, glorious immortals steeped in the power and lifeblood of eternity.

From its conceptual self, the Brahman created all things, starting with Lord Brahma and Lord Vishnu. Thus, were formed two of the three greatest gods. Though other immortals came after, these were the mightiest and most honored.

Vishnu napped on the water, the first object created. The cool waves lulled him to sleep, rocking his greatness on their crests. His skin was blue.

A shining egg appeared in the water, glowing as brightly as the sun. Brahma formed himself within the egg, growing and molding his form for a thousand years. Eventually, Brahma burst from the egg. The two pieces fell apart, creating heaven and earth, respectively. Hidden inside those pieces were the landmasses. Brahma shaped them with his mighty hands, forming the continents from the water.

After he shaped the world, Brahma meditated. From his elevated thoughts sprang ten sons. (Gods aren't always born the same way as men.) These were the sages, the founts of wisdom to whom Brahma revealed his wisdom. Another god, Dharma, emerged from Brahma's mighty chest.

Others tell another story. Lord Vishnu, the protector, and preserver, formed for himself a Chaturbhuj, a form with four arms. Prakriti, the feminine creative force, joined him in his effort. In his arms, he held a lotus flower and his mace, the weapon of justice. From the ocean's waves came Lakshmi, whom Lord Vishnu accepted as his consort.

From his navel grew a lotus flower, and its blossom stretched across the ocean. From the blossom emerged Brahma, the creator, and friend to Vishnu throughout eternity.

Thus began the world of the gods, the dawn of the first beginning.

Chapter 2: The Birth of Lord Shiva

A short time after the creation, Lord Brahma and Lord Vishnu chanced upon each other while walking in an empty plain.

"Greetings, Lord Brahma," said Lord Vishnu, respectfully.

"Greetings, Lord Vishnu," Brahma responded. "Where are you going over this barren plain?"

"I go to look over my greatness," said Lord Vishnu, proudly. "In this world, my devotion takes first importance, and I go to listen to the prayers of my people."

This reply did not please Lord Brahma.

"Many may pray to you, Lord Vishnu," he said, "but they forget whom it was who gave them lips to pray. When they honor you in prayer, they honor me more, since I gave them the ground on which to worship."

Lord Vishnu scowled, and the ground beneath him shook.

"If there be a greater power than I, then let him manifest!"

Between the two gods appeared a blazing pillar that stretched both into the sky and into the depths of the earth. Its light blinded them, and they raised their hands to ward off the glare. They craned their necks back until they touched the earth, yet they could not see the end of the pillar.

Lord Brahma and Lord Vishnu were filled with wonder. Who could be mightier than both the Creator and the Preserver of the world? They decided to seek the end of the pillar.

"I shall change into a goose and seek the end of the pillar in eternity," said Lord Brahma. He stretched out his arms, and they grew great white feathers, and his face narrowed to a goose's thin bill.

"I shall change into a boar and seek the end of the pillar in the earth," said Lord Vishnu. His blue skin changed to matted hair, and his nose grew long, sharp tusks.

Lord Brahma leaped into the sky and Lord Vishnu dove into the earth, both seeking the end of the great pillar without a name.

Lord Brahma beat his wings and soared past the treetops. He beat them again and rose above the hills. He beat them again and floated above the mountains. The pillar stretched higher still. He beat his wings even higher and soared among the heavens. He beat them again and rose among the stars. The pillar stretched higher still. Lord Brahma flew for ages, beyond time and eternity itself, until his wings ached and his feathers drooped with fatigue. Still there was no end to the pillar. He returned to the empty plain.

Lord Vishnu dug deep into the earth, past the roots of plants and trees. He dug further, snuffling his nose deeper, past the roots of rivers. The pillar stretched deeper. He dug deeper, past the feet of mountains. He dug deeper and deeper into the bottom of the earth itself. The pillar stretched farther still. Lord Vishnu dug until his tusks were dulled and his whiskers drooped with fatigue. Still there was no end to the pillar. He returned to the empty plain.

"Lord Brahma!" called Lord Vishnu, when he saw Lord Brahma land on the grasses. "I have dug and dug and cannot find the end of the pillar. It does not end in the earth."

"Ah, Lord Vishnu!" returned Lord Brahma. "I have flown and flown and cannot find the end of the pillar. It does not end in the sky."

The pillar shook, and the earth trembled. It shook again, and the sky shuddered. It shook a third time, and a shining figure stepped from its depths.

His skin was marred with bhasma (ashes), and his head was matted and curly. A third eye called Tryambakam burned in his forehead. A snake hissed at his throat.

He lowered his trident, the trisul. Lord Brahma and Lord Vishnu bowed in acknowledgment. Here truly was a power as great—if not greater—than their own.

Thus was born Lord Shiva, the destroyer, Lord of demons. He made his home in Varanasi, and married Parvati, from whom he was rarely separated. But that is a story for another page.

Chapter 3: Saraswati & Brahma's Fifth Head

After the creation, Brahma looked over the world and was pleased. He saw the water and land, the mountains and hills. He saw the sun, Aditya, whose rays blessed the earth. He saw the sages, sprung from his thought. But none of these beings, as yet, had been born to a mother and father.

So, Lord Brahma drew from his own body a form, half male and half female. The male was called Swayambhu Manu, and the female Shatarupa. We know her better by another name: Saraswati.

Saraswati's dark hair stretched to her waist, and her face was pure and open. In her hands, she held a veena by which to bless the universe with music and wisdom. Hansa, the swan, bore her on his back.

When he saw the beauty of Saraswati, Lord Brahma's soul moved within him. He longed for her as his wife. But Saraswati, drawn from his own body, was like his daughter.

One day she approached Lord Brahma to pay her respects. He gazed at her with intense desire. When she circled behind him, he could see her no longer. So great was his longing that a second head sprouted from behind his first one, the better to gaze on Saraswati and her beauty.

Saraswati passed to Lord Brahma's left, and a third head appeared to gaze at her still. When she passed to his right, yet another—a fourth head—sprouted from his shoulders so she could not escape his sight.

The attention troubled Saraswati. To gain a moment's peace from Brahma's desire, she jumped over his head. A fifth head sprouted from Brahma's shoulders so that Saraswati could find no rest from his interest.

Lord Shiva witnessed the performance and was displeased.

"It is not lawful to pursue your daughter, Lord Brahma," he said. Four of Brahma's heads praised Shiva in agreement. The fifth head hissed and reviled Shiva for his interference. Lord Shiva drew his sword.

"A head that speaks in such a way shall not speak at all."

And so Lord Brahma lost his fifth head that spoke evilly to Lord Shiva. Eventually, Brahma and Saraswati married, and have lived together since. Shatarupa married Swayambhu Manu and produced the first children. Thus began the cycle of fathers and mothers from the first man and woman.

Chapter 4: Shiva Tests Parvati

In the Himalayas there lived a great king. He and his wife, Mena Devi, served Lord Shiva and offered him many respects. But they were unfulfilled. They wished for one thing and one thing only: for a daughter to grow and become the wife of Shiva.

"Oh, that our family could be worthy of this honor!" cried Himavantha, the king. "I am a ruler, yet I am poor as the poorest peasant without this gift."

"Then let us perform a tapasya," answered Mena Devi. "It will please Gauridevi, the wife of Shiva. Perhaps she will be reborn as our daughter."

King Himavantha agreed. Mena Devi began her tapasya. The sun rose and fell, and still, she meditated. The shadows chased themselves across her face, and still she meditated. No food crossed her lips, and no water wet her tongue. Finally, after three days, Guaridevi heard the meditation of Mena Devi.

"I am pleased by your devotion," said Guaridevi. "What do you ask of me?"

"Great goddess," said Mena Devi, bowing herself to the ground. "Himavantha is a great ruler among men, and I am his wife. But our wealth is nothing without a blessing. We wish only to have you as our daughter, and raise you to be the wife of Shiva."

The request pleased Guaridevi.

"I will be reborn as your daughter. Lord Shiva will grieve, but he will find me again."

Guaridevi leaped into a fire. Her form as Gauridevi perished in the flames, and Shiva lamented her loss. Meanwhile, Mena Devi conceived and bore a daughter; she named her Parvati. Her first word was Shiva, and by this, her parents knew that Gauridevi had kept her promise. Parvati grew fairer and wiser every day until she was finally of the age to seek Shiva.

After Guaridevi perished in the flames, Lord Shiva meditated for many years to mourn her loss. He meditated so deeply that he neither heard sound nor saw sights without the depth of his mourning. When the time came for Parvati to wed Shiva, he could neither see nor hear her. The king consulted with Narada, a wise sage.

"What is to be done?" King Himavantha asked. "Our daughter must wed Lord Shiva, but his mind wanders in other paths."

"Lord Shiva is deep in meditation," answered Narada, "but the prayers of worship may still reach his ears. Send Parvati to pray at his shrine, and perhaps he will hear her voice if her devotion is pure."

Himavantha was pleased with this counsel and sent Parvati to the shrine of Lord Shiva. When Parvati's eyes fell on Lord Shiva deep in his meditation, her heart danced within her, and she was determined to offer reverence to none but him. She performed tapasya in his honor and offered him worship by every means within her power. Her devotions did not cease with the night but continued through till the dawn. She prayed until her voice craked and her eyes drooped with fatigue. Deep in his meditation, Lord Shiva heard her prayers.

"This truly is a pure woman," he thought, "who prays and offers worship to me without ceasing. Perhaps I shall take her as my wife."

But first Lord Shiva sought to test Parvati, for perhaps she loved something better than he. He dressed in robes of gold silk and wore the face of a rich Brahmin. Coming to the shrine where Parvati continued to pray, he feigned oblation to Shiva before turning to her.

"Would you waste your devotions at a shrine of no consequence?"

Parvati's eyes flashed, but she did not stop her worship. Lord Shiva hid his smile and tried again.

"Would you wish to live without wealth, with only the ashes as your comfort?"

Parvati turned her back to him and continued to pray, but her hands shook with anger. Lord Shiva was pleased but tested her a third time.

"It would be a pity for a beautiful, rich girl to marry a poor beggar, though he be a god."

Parvati spun around.

"I will marry none but Shiva!"

"I am he."

Lord Shiva cast away his disguise, revealing his true nature. Parvati clapped her hands for joy and fell at his feet. Lord Shiva raised her gently.

"You have proven your devotion. I will take you as my bride."

Himavantha and Mena Devi were overjoyed by Parvati's marriage and blessed the goddess for keeping her promise to them. And so, Lord Shiva and his consort, Parvati were married.

Chapter 5: Shiva Snares a Whale

Lord Shiva undertook to teach his wife Parvati, about the Vedas. They sat down in the garden behind their home, where the flowers bloomed, and the grasses waived in the mountain breeze.

"Listen, Parvati, to the beauty of the Vedas and the wisdom therein," said Lord Shiva. Then he began. He unfolded the gyan, the knowledge, and Parvati listened. The day stretched into a week. He bathed his understanding in the Rig Veda, the Sama Veda, the Yajur Veda, and the Atharva Veda. The week stretched into months. Lord Shiva examined the Samhitas, speaking their mantras and singing their prayers. He revealed the Aranyakas and explained the rituals and ceremonies. The months stretched into years. He reviewed the Brahmanas and their commentaries and meditated over the Upanishads. The years stretched into a thousand years, and the seasons swelled and faded around them like the heartbeat of the earth. Still, Lord Shiva expounded the Vedas and their wisdom and delighted in their words.

Parvati listened. She listened to the mandalas and the meters of the hymns and hummed quietly with them. She listened as the trees stretched their roots deeper into the mountain soil and birds sang their lives away. After many years, her eyes drooped with fatigue, and she yawned.

Lord Shiva frowned. "Have you lost your interest, Parvati?"

"Only for a moment," she replied. "My eyes drooped with fatigue and I yawned without taking thought. I am listening now."

Lord Shiva was displeased.

"Go to earth and take birth as a fisherwoman."

"What have I done to deserve punishment?" Parvati cried.

But Lord Shiva did not reply. He stalked away, and the ash flaked from his skin and the skulls around his neck clicked and clacked in ire. Parvati obeyed. She took the form of a beautiful baby girl, who cried and cried until a fisherman noticed her kicking under a tree. He picked her up and carried her home, for his wife had died, leaving him no children, and he was glad to find one to be his own.

Lord Shiva climbed to the top of his mountain to meditate. He meditated for many years, but when he came to himself again, Parvati was still absent. He traveled to the four mountain faces, and in the glitter of crystal, ruby, gold, and lapis lazuli he saw the beauty of Parvati and her love for him. His heart was heavy then, and he regretted his punishment.

Parvati grew more beautiful every day. She learned to row, and soon rowed the fastest of any other in the village. She learned to fish and assisted her father with his catch. Soon he became the wealthiest man in the village.

Lord Shiva sat by himself on Mount Kailasha. The air was empty without the sound of Parvati's voice; his home was empty without her presence. Lord Shiva sat sadly until his shoulders drooped and his matted hair dragged in the dirt. Nandi, the wise bull upon which Shiva sometimes traveled, saw his master's grief.

"Can you not call Parvati back?" he asked. "I know she would come if you asked her."

"I cannot," said Lord Shiva, and great tears rolled from all three of his eyes. "Parvati's destiny requires her to marry an angler."

And he sighed such a great sigh that the clouds around Mount Kailasha tossed and heaved like a summer storm. Nandi sorrowed when he saw Lord Shiva aching for his wife.

"What can I do to help Lord Shiva?" he wondered. "I must find a way to ease his sadness."

Nandi went to Parvati's village and watched while she rowed and fished with her father. She laughed as the water splashed over the side of the boat and sang with the whisper of the waves.

"Her voice ought to be on Mount Kailasha, not here in a fisher village," thought Nandi. "But since she cannot yet return, perhaps my master can meet her here."

Nandi changed himself into a great whale. His body stretched longer than four fisher boats and his tail gleamed like a waning half-moon. He waited until the fishermen pushed out to the fishing grounds, and then followed their boats stealthily. When they cast their nets to fish, Nandi tangled them in his fins and tore them from the boats. The fishermen lamented their bad luck and cast out new nets. Again, Nandi tangled their nets in his fins and tore them off. The fishermen poked at him with their oars, and he flipped over their boats. Finally, the fishermen gave up and headed back to shore without their catch.

For the next several days Nandi plagued the fishermen. He tangled their nets and tipped their boats. He scared away the fish and made great, rough waves with his tail. Day after day the fishermen went home with empty nets and stomachs. Eventually, their complaints reached the ears of Parvati's father, who was a wealthy leader among them. He listened while they spun the tale of the trickster whale that spoiled their fishing, and then raised his hands for silence.

"He who catches the whale," he said, "will have my daughter as a wife. He must not plague our village anymore."

The fishermen murmured in excitement and set straightaway for their boats. They baited their lines with tasty morsels and stretched large nets between spaces in the rocks. They roamed among the waves, poking the crests with their spears. But none could catch Nandi. He stole their bait, stretched and broke the nets, and escaped the points of the spears. One by one the fishermen turned back. None could catch the whale.

Parvati's father worried for the village if they could procure no food. He prayed to Lord Shiva day and night. Parvati stood by him in his vigil and offered him water when his lips went dry.

"Please Lord, help to rid us of this crafty whale."

He prayed until his eyes drooped with fatigue. Finally, when he could pray no longer, Parvati whispered for him.

"Please, Lord Shiva, hear my father's prayer."

Far away on the top of Mount Kailasha, Shiva heard Parvati's words. They floated on the wind and settled into his heart, and he received them gladly. He transformed himself into a young man and presented himself before Parvati's father.

"I will catch this whale," he said, "and earn the hand of the maiden."

Parvati blushed but smiled at the handsome stranger. Lord Shiva boarded his boat and paddled out to the fishing grounds. Nandi heard the voice of his master and swam nearby. When Lord Shiva cast out his line, Nandi leaped for the hook. When Lord Shiva showed the fisherman that he had caught Nandi, the whale, he was given Parvati to be his wife.

Thus were Lord Shiva and Parvati reunited and Nandi the whale tamed.

Chapter 6: Ganesha Loses His Head

At times Lord Shiva is absentminded. It is a great responsibility to meditate and to chase the negative forces from the world; so great, perhaps, that other obligations is swallowed up in the way.

One day, Lord Shiva approached the hour of his departure. He hugged and kissed his wife fondly.

"I will return shortly," said he, "once the negative forces have been expelled."

Parvati embraced him and wished him good fortune.

"May you find success in your journey and return home without incident."

Lord Shiva went away to meditate. The negative forces were significant at that time, and it required much focus and effort to cast them away.

Parvati waited patiently, but her husband did not return. Soon she began to be big with child. Still, she waited for her husband. When the child was born, she named him Ganesha. He and his sister, Ashoka Sundari, filled Parvati's days with laughter and sunshine and eased the ache of Shiva's absence. Ganesha grew into a healthy boy and helped his mother and sister greatly.

After some years, Lord Shiva shook himself from deep meditation and found that he missed his wife. The negative forces had been dispelled, and he was free to return home. He made the journey as quickly as he could and was surprised to find a man-child standing by the gate. Lord Shiva made to enter the house, and the man-child stopped him.

"You shall not enter into this house," said Ganesha, for he did not recognize his father, who had been absent for so many years. "The goddess is not prepared to receive you."

Lord Shiva smiled and made to brush the boy aside. Ganesha resisted and blocked the way.

"You shall not enter," he repeated. He stood in front of the gate and folded his arms.

Lord Shiva frowned. He did not know that he had left Parvati pregnant with this son.

"How is it that I cannot enter at my own home?" he said. "Move aside, child."

"This is my home, and I do not know you," said Ganesha defiantly, "so you shall not pass."

Lord Shiva was displeased and impatient to see his wife. Without another word, he sliced the head from Ganesha's shoulders and tossed the body to one side. He met Parvati coming from a bath and opened his arms to embrace her. But the body of Ganesha peeped out from the corner of the house, and she fell to her knees, wailing.

"Ah, my son! My Lord, what has happened? My son, my son!"

"Your son?" Lord Shiva said, astonished.

"Our son," replied the goddess, as she cradled Ganesha's body in her arms.

"I knew him not when I arrived," said Lord Shiva, and he told Parvati all he had done. Parvati wept bitterly, and her tears watered the ground. Ganesha's sister wept also as she hid behind a bag of salt. Ever after Asohoka Sundari was linked with the taste of salt, because of her fear of her father and her grief for her brother. To comfort Parvati, Lord Shiva proposed a solution.

"Because he is our son, I may seek for him a new head to put on his shoulders and replace the old one. I will take the head from the first being I find asleep and bring it back from our son, who shall be whole again."

And so Lord Shiva left and searched for a new head Ganesha. He searched in the river, and he searched in the mountain but found no new head for his son among the water and rocks. He searched further still in the jungle below and found a baby elephant sleeping. Lord Shiva plucked off its head and carried it back for Ganesha.

When Parvati saw the heavy elephant head on her little son's shoulders, she cried and cried, but there was nothing more she could do. Lord Brahma and Lord Vishnu blessed the boy and sealed Lord Shiva's gift.

Thus, ever after Ganesha bore the head of an elephant.

Chapter 7: Ganesha Spills a River

Many years ago, Sage Agastya lived in a dry and barren country. The plants wilted, and the cracked earth ached for water. Sage Agastya withdrew himself to a sacred place and prayed mightily to Lord Brahma and Lord Shiva.

"Oh great Lords who offer blessings of peace and cultivation," he said. "Hear the prayers of your humble servant and bless this broken land that your names may be reverenced forever."

The gods heard his prayers. Lord Brahma and Lord Shiva appeared to Sage Agastya.

"What will you?" asked Lord Shiva. The skulls around his neck clicked and clacked together, but Sage Agastya did not fear. He bowed his head.

"Great Lord, give me sacred water to bless this land, that the plants and people may grow strong and well-formed."

"It shall be done," Shiva replied. "Bring forth your kamandalu, and I shall fill it."

Sage Agastya brought forth his little water pot and offered reverence to Lord Brahma and Lord Shiva. Lord Shiva poured into the kamandalu the purest of liquid, the sacred water necessary to start a river. Sage Agastya thanked Lord Shiva and carried the kamandalu away.

He traveled many days over the land, seeking the best place to start the new river. Some hills were too high. Some valleys were too low. Finally, he made his way to the Coorg Mountains. Their green heads brushed the clouds. He sat down on a rock to rest, cradling the kamandalu filled with sacred water in his arms. After a short time, a small boy came down the path.

"Young child," called Sage Agastya. "Will you hold my kamandalu while I relieve myself?"

"Yes, Sage Agastya," said the boy, smiling. "I will hold it."

"Take care," said the sage. "It is filled with sacred water, and it is dangerous to spill."

"I will take care, Sage Agastya."

Sage Agastya gave the boy the kamandalu and went away directly to relieve himself. Once he was gone, the boy laughed and set the kamandalu on the ground. The boy was Ganesha, son of Lord Shiva, and he thought that valley perfect for a new river. The water would spill down from the high places and wash the feet of the mountains below.

When Sage Agastya returned, he was annoyed to see the boy sitting on the rock and the kamandalu sitting on the ground.

"You have neglected the sacred water!" he scolded. "Look, here comes a crow to sully it with his beak. Shoo!"

But the crow did not fly away. He looked at Sage Agastya, and then bent his beak to take some water. Sage Agastya beat the air with his arms, scaring the crow away. The crow's claws caught the edge of the kamandalu, spilling the sacred water. Immediately a river sprang up and rushed down the mountainside.

Thus was born the River Kaveri, the sacred river prayed for by Sage Agastya, gifted by Lord Shiva, planned by Ganesha, and spilled by a crow.

Chapter 8: Kubera's Pride

On an important festival day Kubera, Lord of the Yakshas, held a feast. His host delivered silk napkins to every guest. The servers carried fine toasted fish and biryani, and chahou kheer porridge steamed in golden bowls. Prestigious guests crossed the threshold. Varuna arrived with his consort Varuni, and her hair glittered with sparkling seashells. Tvastr, the heavenly builder, bowed to Indra, the king of the gods. Though Lord Shiva and Parvati could not attend, they sent their son, Ganesha, as their representative. It was a feast of decadence, and Kubera soaked in the glory of his wealth.

The guests sat down to eat, and all were pleased with the spread. Varuna praised the amritsari fish while Varuni tasted sweet imarti. Tvastr supped savory dal, and dum aloo and Indra relished milky shahi paneer. Their cups were full, and the guests laughed and joked on plush rugs and pillows.

Lord Ganesha consumed the rajma beans and naan bread. He devoured samosa and tandoori chicken. He demolished balls of pani puri and pots of palak paneer. The decadent feast disappeared, one golden platter at a time. The other guests halted their discussion and watched as each dish slipped down Ganesha's empty throat. He devoured the dishes, the napkins, and the tablecloth. He swallowed the candles, the singers and dancers, and even the tables and seats; the host's flailing arms and gold-shod feet slipped away as Ganesha swallowed him whole.

"Please, Great One!" Kubera cried again. "Spare my people!"

But instead, Ganesha swallowed the plump pillows and ornate tapestries. He swallowed the candles and the kamandalu, and the water sloshed in his great stomach.

"Stop, Lord Ganesha!" cried Kubera horrified. "Let your hunger be appeased!"

But Lord Ganesha did not stop. He swallowed and swallowed until all of Alakapuri, the city of Kubera, trembled in terror. Kubera placed his swiftest shoes on his feet and ran to Lord Shiva's home on Mount Kailash. He sprinted past the rivers feeding the grass as they wound on their way. He ran past the hills where the cattle and elephants grazed. He ran to the mountains where the birds sang sweetly and fed upon the rich fruit and berries.

Finally, he arrived at the home of Lord Shiva, where the great lord and his consort, Parvati, sat eating a simple meal.

"Lord Shiva! Hear my pleadings and cause Ganesha to cease devouring," Kubera said, falling at Lord Shiva's feet. "My city shakes, and my people tremble in fear because of his ceaseless hunger."

Lord Shiva said nothing but smiled a little as he stood. From his table he lifted a cup of plain, roasted grains, and carried it back to Alakapuri, walking calmly the whole way. Kubera followed, wondering perhaps if it had been a mistake to consult Lord Shiva after all.

When they arrived, Ganesha had torn the doors off their hinges and swallowed them whole. Lord Shiva handed Ganesha the cup of roasted grains.

"Ah," sighed Ganesha, restfully. "I am appeased."

Ganesha's hunger for food ceased, and he sat quietly on the bare ground. Kubera bowed his head in shame.

"Forgive my weakness, Lord Shiva. I saw only my wealth and not the good purposes for which it might be used. In my eyes, the gold of plate and fork glittered more brightly than the eyes of my people. I am reproved."

Thus, Ganesha consumed the sumptuous feast, and Kubera learned his prideful mistake.

Chapter 9: Ganesha Injures a Goddess

Once, when Lord Ganesha was in his infancy, he found a shabby housecat in a village near his home. The cat curled under a set of worn wooden stairs, and dust marred her coat.

"Come play with me!" Little Lord Ganesha commanded the cat. It slunk further into the shadows and hid its eyes with its striped tail. Lord Ganesha was displeased and pulled the cat out from under the porch by her hind leg. He swung her into the air and caught her again, and then threw her high in the air to see how many times she could land on her feet. The poor cat was soon tired and covered in bruises. Lord Ganesha tired of his game and went to Mount Kailash to meet his mother for lunch.

When he arrived home, the house was quiet. Lord Ganesha poked his head through the door. His mother was not in the kitchen. He passed to the back of the house and entered the garden. His mother was not there. He walked through the halls and found her huddled in a corner, covered in deep, purple bruises.

"Mother!" cried Lord Ganesha, running to her side. "What has happened?"

"You hurt me, child." Parvati sighed deeply. "When you tossed me in the air, I fell to the ground and bruised myself."

"But Mother," said Lord Ganesha, anxious to reassure her. "I did not throw you in the air. I have only just arrived home."

"I was the cat you tossed in the village below. It was my coat you dirtied, my tail you tweaked, and my sides that you bruised."

Parvati winced and paused to take her breath. Lord Ganesha bowed his head in shame.

"Mother, I am grieved. I know now that to injure another for entertainment is wrong and hurtful."

Great tears slipped from Lord Ganesha's eyes, and his tears moistened the floorboards near his mother's feet.

"It is a good lesson, child," said Parvati, rising. Lord Ganesha helped her to the kitchen and set before her a healing and hearty repast. Thus Lord Ganesha learned mercy and kindness to those smaller than he.

Chapter 10: Ganesha Wins a Race

Lord Ganesha and his brother, Karthikeya were very competitive. They jumped off stones to see who could leap the highest. They threw stones into the river to see who could splash the farthest. They even measured themselves against the trees to see who was the tallest.

One day, the gods gave the children a piece of special fruit from the gods. Its leaves were like fronds of silk, and its flesh was as delicious and milky as the cream from a cow. Both boys desired the fruit.

"It is mine!" cried Karthikeya. "I am the hungriest!"

"It is mine!" cried Ganesha. "I am the largest and need the most feeding!"

The boys fought until their parents separated them. Lord Shiva sought to restore peace.

"My children, you could share the fruit. Then both could taste its sweetness and be filled."

Lord Ganesha looked at Karthikeya. Karthikeya looked at Lord Ganesha.

"No!" they screamed together. "It is mine!"

Parvati sighed, but Lord Shiva smiled.

"Very well. Since you do not desire to share, each of you may have the opportunity to win the fruit. The first child to round the world three times wins the prize."

Karthikeya laughed and called his glorious peacock. Its feathers flashed once in the sunlight, and then Karthikeya and the peacock were gone, flying into the horizon.

Lord Ganesha sadly called his mount—the little mouse—and climbed on its back. The mouse ran as fast as it could, but it was tiny, and Lord Ganesha was very heavy. They had only gone a few feet before the mouse needed to stop for a rest. They travelled like that—the mouse and Lord Ganesha—for some time. After awhile, Lord Ganesha heard beating wings and turned as Karthikeya flew past.

"Ha, Brother!" Karthikeya cried, waving a stray peacock feather. "You might as well turn back. My mount is by far the fastest, and I will surely win the fruit!"

And Karthikeya's peacock disappeared again into the sky. Lord Ganesha sighed and turned his mouse toward home, sad already for the lost prize and Karthikeya's gloating.

As he neared home, he saw his parents—Lord Shiva and Parvati—waiting near the gate. A sudden idea occurred to him.

"Mother and Father," he said as he approached them. "May I round you three times since you are my world?"

Parvati smiled, and Lord Shiva nodded. Ganesha, on his little mouse, rounded his parents once. The little mouse stopped to rest. He rounded them twice. Karthikeya flapped by on his peacock and crowed his forthcoming victory. Lord Ganesha rounded his parents the third time.

Lord Shiva handed Lord Ganesha the fruit and blessed him for his insight. When Karthikeya arrived, he watched with a long face as the fruit disappeared into Lord Ganesha's stomach. Thus, Karthikeya earned his reward for gloating, and Lord Ganesha earned his for his wisdom.

Chapter 11: Shiva Skips Success

When Lord Ganesha was a small boy, Lord Shiva issued an important declaration on his son's behalf. Those who wished for success in any effort must first pay homage to Lord Ganesha. When a farmer strove in his fields and wished to bring in his harvest, he must reverence Lord Ganesha. When a servant sought a boon from his master, he must reverence Lord Ganesha.

"In no way may any receive success except by Lord Ganesha," he decreed. And it was so. Merchants offered prayers over their goods. Fathers prayed over their daughters and sons as they went forth to their marriages, and mothers prayed over their daughters as they brought forth children. All those who prayed to Lord Ganesha received success in their endeavors, and the name of Lord Ganesha was much loved.

Eventually, the demons in Tripura rose up in rebellion. They cursed the name of Shiva and threatened mortals and gods. Lord Shiva gathered his forces, bid farewell to his family, and started on his way. His forces marched for many days, and Lord Shiva bore his trident at their head. His mighty carriage rolled forth on the way to battle.

One day, Lord Shiva rode in his chariot, pondering over the upcoming battle. Crack! The carriage shook and jilted, throwing Lord Shiva awry. His soldiers ran to see what was the matter and lo! One of the pegs in the wheel had snapped.

"Ah!" said Lord Shiva. "It is just. For a while I decreed that all should pay homage to my son before success, I neglected my own words and did not offer my reverence as I ought."

Then Lord Shiva prayed to Lord Ganesha for success in his endeavor and gave repentance for his thoughtlessness. The soldiers of Lord Shiva fixed the peg and continued on their journey.

When they arrived in Tripura, the demons were many and restless. Their forms were dark and terrible, and their defiance set. Lord Shiva and his forces fought bravely and surely and turned the tide of the battle. The demons were subdued, and Lord Shiva returned home in safety.

Thus, Lord Shiva learned to honor his own word with the same homage that he paid to his son.

Chapter 12: Ravana's Ten Heads

There once was a scholar who was more learned than any other. He spent years mastering the Vedas and the Shastras and explored the mysteries of the universe. He plucked the veena until it played like the sound of a thousand birds singing. He wrote complex works about the stars that moved in the heavens and the medicine necessary to prolong life. He studied and learned until there was no theory left for him to master. But still, he was both mortal and vulnerable. He decided to seek a boon from the gods.

He meditated standing on one toe, and although wind and the rain smote him to and fro, he did not move. Still, the gods were silent. He fasted for a thousand years, long enough to forget the taste of food and the freshness of water. Still, his tapasya was unheard. Finally, he began to slice off his heads, and with each head lost part of himself.

He sliced off the first head, and with it sacrificed the ahamkara, the love of one's self. The great head, matted with dark hair, rolled to the ground and settled near his feet. Still, the gods were silent. Another head sprouted in its place, and Ravana raised his sword to strike again.

He sliced off the second head, and out came moha, attachment to family and friends. Still, the heavens were silent, and a new head sprouted to replace the one lost.

He sliced off the third head and released the love of his perfect self, which led to paschyataap, penance or repentance.

He sliced off the fourth head and loosed krodha, the rage that causes harm in others.

He sliced off the fifth head and forewent ghrina, the burning hatred.

He sliced off the sixth head and surrendered bhaya, the terror of possibility.

He sliced off the seventh head and offered up irshya, the sting of jealousy.

He sliced off the eighth head and abandoned lobha, the greed for possessions.

He sliced off the ninth head and relinquished kama, the heat of lust.

He sliced off the tenth head and forfeited jaddata, the pull of inaction or inertia.

At last, ten heads lay piled at Ravana's feet, and he sat back, exhausted. He had nothing else to offer. Lord Brahma appeared next to the pile of mangled offerings. He greeted Ravana respectfully.

"Ravana, I have heard your oblations and accept them. Do you seek a boon from me?"

"Haan ji, Lord Brahma," said Ravana, and he bowed himself to the ground. "I have sought power in the Vedas and the Shastras, and in great learning. But still, I am vulnerable. I wish to be made immortal and to become as one of the gods."

Lord Brahma heard and sighed, shaking his head.

"Though your penance and learning were both profound, Ravana, this gift is beyond my inclination to give. However, I will make you a promise that will cover in part your vulnerability: no god or demon will have the power to seek your life."

Ravana smiled. "This boon I will seek."

And when he had spoken his words, the ten heads of Ravana revived and grew more swart and tough than before. The sprouted anew from his broad shoulders, and arms spring out to serve them. Ravana took up arms and became the king of the rakshasas (the maneaters who plagued Lord Brahma at the beginning of the world).

Thus, Ravana became the greatest terror on the earth and in the heaven and ravaged the home of the gods.

Chapter 13: The Birth of Rama

Ravana, king of the rakshasas, terrorized the world. He made war on the mortal realms, slaying the people and seizing their riches and lands. He even distressed the gods and threatened to oust them from their prominence, for Lord Brahma had promised that god or demon could never slay him.

As Ravana's ravages spread, the gods appeared in council before Lord Brahma. Lord Indra, the god of highest heaven and wielder of storms, turned his face to the others.

"We have seen, o holy ones, the terror of Ravana, king of the rakshasas. He has destroyed our people and our shrines and threatens to destroy the footings of heaven itself."

The other gods murmured among themselves. Their worry broke like a wave over the feet of Lord Indra.

"This threat," he continued, "concerns all gods and demons who do not wish to pay homage to Ravana, nor forfeit the world to his hunger. But he is beyond our ability to injure. The sun shields his rays in fear of Ravana. The fire itself shrinks from the footsteps of Ravana. What, then, must be done?"

Lord Brahma sighed and was grieved by the suffering of men and gods, for Lord Brahma is the creator, and cares much for his creations.

"It is true that many are afflicted, and suffer greatly at the hands of Ravana. It is also true that he is protected by a boon he sought and now abuses."

The gods moaned and cast down their heads. Lord Brahma meditated within himself.

"Perhaps," he continued thoughtfully, "we may yet find a way to slay Ravana and cast his influence out. Though he did supplicate a boon of protection from me and though neither god nor demon may harm him, yet a man born of woman escapes those conditions."

Then hope infused the gods, for they saw not all was lost. Just then came Lord Vishnu, bearing his mace and discus and clothed in robes of saffron. His mount, the mighty eagle, alighted near Lord Brahma. The other gods did him reverence and welcomed him with gladness.

"Why, my friends, have I been prayed here? What task is there for me to do on behalf of the world?"

The gods explained their anxiety and the depravity of Ravana. Lord Vishnu's brow knit with concern.

"Lord Brahma, I have heard of the plague of Ravana and the horror of his ravishings. I will descend to the earth and become a man, that I may cast down Ravana and end the swath of his atrocity."

Then the gods rejoiced again as hope burned yet brighter. Truly Lord Vishnu, the great Madhava, and protector of worlds, could save them from the vexation of Ravana.

Then the Maruts, the winds, brought Indra tidings.

"A great king among men supplicated for a son," they said. "Dasaratha, this king, seeks knowledge and blessings from Brahma, the creator of all."

Lord Brahma nodded approvingly.

"Lord Vishnu shall descend to the family of Dasaratha and bless him with four sons. These sons shall defend both heaven and the world and bring an end to Ravana and his armies."

Lord Vishnu bowed his acceptance. The gods sent a messenger to Dasaratha, who was overjoyed to receive so honored a son. To prepare his wives to bear the sacred children, the gods sent a vase filled with holy nectar. Queen Kausalya consumed half, and Queen Sumitra and Queen Kaikeyi consumed a quarter each.

Thus Queen Kausalya conceived a bore Rama, the hero of the world.

Chapter 14: Urmila's Slumber

Rama, the son of Dasaratha and Kausalya, grew great in knowledge of war and wisdom. The time came for Dasaratha to choose between his sons and ordain which would follow him on the throne and lead the people in peace. Manthara, the waiting woman of Kaikeyi, spun dark and twisted tales of betrayal and destruction once Rama received the crown. Kaikeyi and her child, Bharata, would be ousted, she said. If she wished to escape destruction for her and her line, she must place Bharata first, even before Shatrughna and Lakshman. The young queen appeared before King Dasaratha.

"My Lord," she said, and her heart resounded with Manthara's twisted words. "Many years ago, you promised me a boon that I never received. I ask it now. Place Bharata on the throne, that he may be king after you and lead our people to peace."

Then King Dasaratha sorrowed because his heart ached for Rama and his leadership.

"Would you ask me this boon when you know it cost me my heart to bestow it?"

Queen Kaikeyi would not rescind her request, thanks to the whispers of Manthara, and so the king was bound to keep his word. Accordingly, Bharata was anointed king, and Rama sent into exile for fourteen years. Tormented by his promise, King Dasaratha died of a broken heart. Bharata refused to rule and placed Rama's silk slippers on the throne instead, in preparation for the day when the true king would return to bless the people.

All grieved when they heard the fruit of Manthara's wicked words. Rama bore the sad news to his lovely wife, Sita.

"My dear," said he. "We must forsake the riches and privilege of my father's palace, for I am bound to obey his commands. We will live in the jungle, in exile, until we may return once again to our home in Ayodhya."

Sita smiled, and her beauty glowed like the sun. She kissed her husband.

"I am not afraid," she said. "I will go with you."

Then Lakshman, the brother of Rama, mourned even more deeply. He would not be parted from Rama, even in exile.

"I wish to protect him if I can," Lakshman told his wife. "At least from some of the dangers of the jungle I may shield him if I accompany him into exile."

"Then go," said Urmila, the wife of Lakshman. "It is honorable to defend the son of Kausalya and even more honorable still to join him in trial as well as pleasure."

"But how will I protect him from harm?" asked Lakshman. "I am, but one man and the dangers of the jungle do not sleep."

"I will sleep on your behalf," said Urmila, "that you may dedicate both day and night to the protection of Rama and Sita."

Lakshman kissed his wife in gratitude and made preparations to leave. When the son of Kausalya left his home in Ayodhya, Lakshman went with them, bidding his faithful wife farewell.

Thus for fourteen years he guarded Rama and Sita, and passed with them through jungle, danger, battle, and death; and, for fourteen years

Urmila slept on her couch in Ayodhya, that her husband might fulfill his duty.

Chapter 15: Deer of Deception

For many years Rama lived in the jungle with his beloved Sita and his brother, Lakshman, waiting to return to Ayodhya and regain his rightful crown. They fetched fruit from the trees and wove baskets from the fronds. The days Rama and Sita spent in happiness in each other's company, and the nights they spent under the watchful eye of Lakshman, who guarded them faithfully. Their friend, Jatayu, the eagle, kept watch for them also.

After a little more than thirteen years, Sita went to fetch water one day and noticed a mysterious deer. His antlers sparkled, and his coat shone with gold flecks. Sita tried to go after it, but the deer skittered away.

"Rama," said Sita, coming with the water jug and pointing to the trees. "A deer of gold runs in the fringe of the wood. He is beautiful, and his coat shines like polished gold."

Rama looked to the trees and spied the deer grazing near the roots. His heart shifted within him, and he frowned.

"I do not look kindly on this deer, my Sita. My heart is ill at ease that he should appear so near to our house and tempt you after him."

"But is he not beautiful?" Sita insisted. "I wish that you would get him for me."

Rama hesitated.

"I do not like him, either, Lord Rama," said Lakshman, eying the deer with his bow on his shoulder, ever ready to defend Rama and Sita. "My heart, too, sits ill when I look over his beauty, great as it is."

Sita sighed and looked after the deer longingly. She had not asked for riches, nor for privilege in her exile, though she was a queen among women. Rama looked upon his wife and ached for her disappointment. He forgot the warning in his heart and sought only to please Sita.

"I will fetch the deer," he said, stringing his bow, "to please Sita and to bring her a gift. If there be any evil about this deer, it is my duty to address it."

Lakshman made to accompany Rama, to protect him in the forest. Rama held up his hand.

"Stay, my brother, while I seek this deer. Would I leave Sita here alone and unprotected?"

"It is my wish to accompany you," said Lakshman, still watching the mysterious deer. "I fear the forest and the temptings of this golden creature."

"I am grateful, my brother," said Rama. "But my life is empty if my Sita is not safe. I will not venture far, and will return shortly."

Then, Lakshman, ill at ease, took up guard outside the cottage of Rama and Sita, and Rama pursued the deer into the woods. The deer darted between trees and around twisted roots, obscuring Rama's shots and drawing him deeper into the forest. Finally, Rama launched a shaft that lodged in the deer, and it stumbled to the ground.

But when Rama approached, the deer revealed himself as Maricha, the demon, who laughed at Rama for his deception.

"Ha! Prince of Ayodhya with no more sense than a beetle! My work is done well, and your precious Sita is lost."

Before Rama could reply, Maricha cried out in voice of Rama.

"Help! Help! I perish! O, Sita! O Lakshman!"

At the cottage, the cries of Maricha sunk into Sita's heart.

"Oh, my husband!" she cried. "Go, Lakshman, and aid him, lest he die alone in the darkness of the jungle!"

"There are none who may harm Rama when he is armed with manavastra, his magic bow," said Lakshman, though his face was worried. Sita was not appeased.

"Oh, go quickly, Lakshman, lest I lose my husband and king both!"

Reluctantly, Lakshman obeyed and set off for the jungle. Then Sita was left alone, and her worries preyed upon her.

"Oh my husband, my Rama! Would that he is safe!"

She prayed many prayers in the cottage, waiting for Lakshman and Rama to return. The sound of footsteps tapped against her ears, and she ran to the door. It was only a poor beggar, seeking alms from the beautiful princess. Sita sighed in disappointment but ran inside to seek alms for the beggar.

As she placed the alms in his hand, he grasped her arm like the grip of death. She cried out and struggled but Ravana, who was the beggar in disguise, only laughed and pulled her to his flying chariot.

"Now you shall be my wife and not the wife of a poor beggar who can neither preserve nor protect you."

"O, Rama! O Lakshman!" Sita screamed as she was born into the air. Jatayu, the eagle, tried to interfere but was cut down by Ravana. Sita, weeping, was born away to Lanka, the island of Ravana, and many nights spent Rama seeking her and pining her loss.

Thus perished Maricha, the trickster demon who deceived Rama and aided Ravana.

Chapter 16: Hanuman's Torch

All were horrified by Sita's captivity. The birds cried out in the canopies and told tales of her beauty and abduction. The monkeys and bears aided Rama in his search, seeking Sita on mountains, in rivers, and over hills. Even Hanuman, the son of Vayu, helped Rama. It was he who finally found Sita imprisoned in the fortress of Ravana.

Hanuman, son of the wind, stood with the army of Rama and looked across the sea to the island of Lanka. There sat the fortress of Ravana, and there, too, sat Sita, imprisoned somewhere inside. How Rama ached for his wife! They had searched for many days and nights without food or rest, and now an impassable ocean divided him and his Sita.

Hanuman was moved with pity for Rama.

"Oh, that I could seek Sita across the waves! How gladly would I fly to her aid for Rama's sake!"

Jambavantha, the bear king, spoke.

"Hanuman, you have forgotten your heritage and abilities. As a child, you plagued the sages and distracted them from their meditations. To preserve their peace, they cursed you with forgetfulness. You are the son of Vayu, the wind, and may fly as he does if you wish."

Then the curse was lifted from Hanuman, and the memory of his abilities surged in him. He heaped from the shore with a scream and soared over the waves to the fortress of Ravana.

He landed near the gates and forced his way past the door guard, but nowhere could he find Sita, whom he knew only by description. He passed the beauties of Ravana's court. Sita was not there. He passed the banquet halls and dark dungeons. Sita was not there, either. Despairing, Hanuman hopped from tree to tree in the gardens. The sound of weeping touched his ears. Under the trees and heavy blossoms, he found Sita, worn thin with worry and the pang of her captivity. She wept for Rama even as fierce demons chastised and abused her.

The sight tore at Hanuman's heart. He waited until an opportune moment and then approached Sita.

"Beautiful princess of Mithila, have hope! Deliverance is soon at hand."

But Sita turned away from him. Too well she knew the torments and false encouragement from the servants of Ravana and suspected Hanuman as another of these. But Hanuman was determined to do her service, if he may. He dropped a shining ring into Sita's hand.

"Look, fair Sita, upon the ring given to you by your faithful husband, Rama. I have brought it as proof both of his devotion and my authenticity as his messenger."

Then Sita smiled and wiped away her tears. She thanked Hanuman for his comfort in her distress. The demons that guarded her returned at this moment and strove with Hanuman. Sita cried out and prayed for his protection. Hanuman fought valiantly, though outnumbered, and caused the demons much anxiety; at length, he was captured and dragged before Ravana.

Hanuman could almost admire the ten-headed sage, so great and marvelous was his court. Then he thought of Rama's grief, and of Sita's tear-stained face.

"What do you here, spy?" asked Ravana gruffly. "Do you come as an emissary from Indra?"

"No," said Hanuman boldly. "I come on behalf of Rama, the prince of Ayodhya, whose wife you have stolen in the basest of crimes. In his name, I demand her return."

"Rama? Ha!" laughed Ravana. "I have stolen what I deserve and recognize no claim from a prince of men."

"Then face your own destruction," said Hanuman. "For though you are immune to both gods and demons, by a man you might yet be killed, and Rama will surely do so unless you return his wife."

Then Ravana called for the death of Hanuman. Ravana's advisors counseled him vigorously, warning him against further unconscionable action.

"Very well," said Ravana. "I will punish him fit for his station. The tail is dearest to a monkey. Burn it!"

The cruel demons shrieked with joy and hurried to carry out the dark order. They wrapped Hanuman's tail with fuel and dragged him through the streets, mocking him and his mission. Then the prayer of Sita intervened on his behalf. Though his tale burned, the heat did not mar him. The flames flickered brightly but did not consume him. Then Hanuman caused his tail to grow until it crackled as merrily as a torch.

"I will leave the mark of Rama," he thought, "and inflict their punishment upon themselves."

Then Hanuman leaped to the rooftops, escaping his captors. He sprung from eave to eave, passing his tail over house and tree. The flames grasped the city until all but Sita's bower was smothered in smoke. Then Hanuman dipped his tail in the ocean, and the waves extinguished the flames.

Thus Hanuman torched Lanka and carried Rama's ultimatum to Ravana, Sita's captor.

Chapter 17: Suvannamachha Steals a Bridge

When Hanuman returned, he told Rama of his exploits and why the smoke floated on the horizon. He assured the prince that Sita was safe and that Ravana would not release her for any prize or persuasion. Rama sorrowed. But the armies of King Jambavantha and the brethren of Hanuman cried out for justice, and both the smoke of ravaged Lanka and the cries of his friends cheered Rama's heart.

"We must rescue my beloved and release her from her torment," said Rama. "But how can we pass over this great water? We have no ships to sail, and the distance is too far to swim."

"Lord Rama, petition Varuna," offered Lakshman. "Surely the lord of the ocean will hear us and help to make a way."

And so Rama prayed, but Varuna would not hear his prayers for fear of Ravana. After some persuasion, Varuna offered the services of an architect serving in his army. Nala could build a bridge to carry Rama's army across the waves. Under Nala's direction, the troops uprooted trees and boulders and tossed them into the sea. Throngs of bears hurled boulders into the sea to form the footings of the bridge. One by one, the rocks crashed into the waves, raising the foundations that much higher.

After a day of effort, the armies noticed a disturbing trend. No matter how many rocks sunk beneath the waves, the bridge progressed no further. The bears sought larger boulders, and the monkeys uprooted greater trees. But the bridge did not advance.

"There is trickery here," said Lakshman, watching the waves. "Something flickers in the depths."

Hanuman stepped forward.

"Send me beneath the waves, Lord Rama," he said. "I will seek the trickster and remove the barriers."

Lord Rama agreed, and Hanuman marched into the waves. He pushed through the water, down deeper and deeper to the ocean floor. Finally, he saw movement in the depths and hid behind a rock to watch.

A troop of enchanting mermaids flitted near the footings of the bridge. When a new boulder descended to the depths, they hauled it away. A mermaid even lovelier than her cohorts watched the process, directing their efforts.

"So!" thought Hanuman angrily. "The bridge does not progress because of these minions, no doubt sent by Ravana to prevent Rama's crossing."

The Hanuman burst from behind his boulder and swam toward the most beautiful, scattering the others in his path.

As he pursued her, Hanuman noticed the mermaid's beauties—the caress of her hair in the current, the flash of her eyes like the sun on the sea.

"Who are you?" he asked, stung by the pangs of love and forgetting the bridge for a moment.

"Suvannamachha," she replied, and her voice was like the echo of bells. "I am the daughter of Ravana."

Then Hanuman remembered his mission and the army hampered by her interference.

"Though my heart aches for you, fair mermaid, yet I am bound to a more serious task. Ravana has captured the wife of Rama and holds her captive on Lanka. It is to rescue her that we construct this bridge."

Then Suvannamaccha was grieved by her father's doings and blessed the construction of the bridge. Her mermaids returned the rocks they had removed, and the bridge progressed again. Hanuman stayed with her for a short time before he returned to the surface. When Savannamaccha bid him goodbye, her eyes returned his love.

"Farewell, son of Vayu, and most handsome of the monkey race. Me and my helpers will guard the bridge from below, so no other may hinder its progress."

Then Hanuman returned to the shore, and Lord Rama congratulated him on his success. Ever after the heart of Hanuman remembered the voice of a beauty beneath the sea.

After five days, the bridge reached Lanka, and the army passed to dry ground at last.

So was built Rama Setu, Rama's Bridge, with the help of Suvannamachha, the daughter of Ravana.

Chapter 18: Hanuman Moves a Mountain

When the bears and monkeys reached Lanka, they pounded the walls of the city with their fists.

"Ha!" said mighty Ravana, and his mouth gaped open like a chasm. "I do not fear these monkeys. I will keep Sita as my own, though it costs me the city of Lanka and everything in it."

His generals and advisors saw the bears and monkeys assaulting the walls, and their nerves trembled with the shaking stones.

"Return Sita, Great Lord!" they cried. "The vultures already circle your capital. The omens predict your downfall. Undo your evil deed and save our beautiful city!"

"Silence!" cried Ravana. "I will not return Sita, after all, I have sacrificed to get and keep her. I will destroy Rama and his armies as easily as the wind strips the leaves from trees!"

Then Ravana's counselors trembled and were silent. Vibhishana, the brother of Ravana, found him deaf to good counsel, and followed dharma to the camp of Rama, seeking refuge. But Ravana cared not. Driven nearly mad by his desire for Sita and restrained by Brahma's curse, he simmered in her rejection and thought of nothing else.

When the forces outside the gate cried for battle, Ravana prepared to deliver it. He sent his greatest generals. Indrajit rode to battle in his war chariot, followed by his brother, Prahasta. Trishira rode forth without fear, all three of his heads cursing Rama and Lakshman for their audacity.

When the two forces clashed, the sound was like mountains crumbling into one another. Rakshasha, monkey, and bear clawed and tore at the enemy, littering the battlefield with the dead and wounded. In the name of Ravana Dhumraksha, Akampana, and Kumbhakarna strode into the melee, and their steps shook the ground. But Hanuman, Angada, Nila, and Nala returned the arrows of the accursed, and massacred Ravana's generals one by one. So dire was the battle that Rama and Lakshman were struck down. Finally, the forces retreated, and the armies were left to sort among the fallen.

Among the wounded, the forces of Rama found Jambavantha, the bear king.

"Hanuman!" he cried. "Where is Hanuman?"

"How do you cry for Hanuman before seeking first after Rama's safety?" asked Vibhishana.

"Only Hanuman can save Rama and Lakshman, for if I have fallen, so surely have they, too."

Then Hanuman was called and came to the bear king.

"What would you, good king?" he asked. "Rama and Lakshman are wounded, and I would help them if I could."

"Listen," said the king. "In the Himalayas, there is a mountain called Mahodaya, the home of sweet herbs and healing. On the slopes, you will find the herbs growing, caressed by the breath of heaven. Return with them quickly that Lakshman and Rama might be healed."

With a great cry, Hanuman sprang into the sky. Quick as the wind he brushed the treetops of the sprawling forests and skipped across the sands of the vast deserts. He bowed in reverence as he passed Mount Kailash, the home of Shiva, but too quickly did he fly to offer any obeisance more. Finally, his toes touched the hallowed mountain. But oh! Thousands of plants covered the mountainside. Which were the ones that might heal Rama and Lakshman? Hanuman dashed from flower to flower, sniffing each by turn.

"The Prince of Ayodhya suffers, and I cannot help him!" cried Hanuman. "Mount Mahodaya, aid me in my search!"

But the mountain was silent. The words of Hanuman echoed off the boulders and bounced back to his face.

"So be it!" he shouted. "If you will not help me, I will take you along!"

Then Hanuman seized the mountaintop and held it like a platter, passing back over desert and forest until he reached the island of Lanka. No sooner had the mountaintop passed over the sea than the breezes wafted over the injured princes and healed their wounds. Jambavantha, too, and the other warriors of Rama's forces received strength and praised the great deed of Hanuman.

Thus, were Rama and Lakshman saved, and the mountaintop of Mayodaya was removed.

Chapter 19: The Final Battle

One by one, the great generals of Lanka were defeated. The kinsmen of Ravana perished under the arrows of Rama. His sons fell to the lance of Lakshman. When Indrajit and his magnificent chariot were conquered, Ravana's rage knew no bounds. He tore the tapestries from his walls and threw down the gold and jewels from their sconces. In his fury, he donned his armor and sword and sought Sita's life, she for whom he had suffered so much.

On his way to her bower, he met one of his advisors, who counseled him.

"Lord Ravana," he said, "There is still yet time and opportunity for you to avenge your sons and kinsmen. The princes of Ayodhya still live, waiting to receive your wrath."

Then the rage of Ravana turned from Sita and toward Rama and his army. "They desecrate the shores of Lanka with their feet and provoke my anger with their defiance!" he cried. "I will descend and finish them personally."

Then the great chariot of Ravana rolled forth as a tongue of fire, and the bears and monkeys quailed before it. Rama saw him come and called to him across the field of shattered spears and broken foes.

"Ravana!" he said, brandishing his bow. "You are come to be punished for your heinous deed, the capture of my wife. But not only this act hangs over you. The fruits of your wrath—the assaults against the sages and Devas—have gone unanswered. Today you are accountable, and the reckoning will be swift."

Ravana hurled his scorn into the face of Rama with a laugh.

"I fear no god nor Deva, as none may harm me. As for Sita, I took only what I deserved, since I found her alone and unguarded by those who should have been her protectors. She is my conquest, and I claim her as my own."

The heart of Rama sickened with grief and indignation, but he answered calmly.

"I am no god nor Deva, but a man—a man whose wife you have stolen. Since you will not return her, I will lay you to waste and seek her myself."

Then Ravana's blood ran cold, and he realized how craftily he had been lured and how blindly his pride had guided him. But even now he would not be swayed, for the thought of Sita and the agony of defeat goaded him.

"Then come," he cried, "and meet your death."

Ravana jumped on his chariot and ordered his charioteer to run Rama down. Hanuman sprang to Rama's side.

"If it please you, Great Lord," he said, humbly. "Ride on my back that you and the demon king might fight on equal footing."

Then Rama blessed him and rode to battle on the back of Hanuman. The conflict rocked the island of Lanka. The astras, the weapons of the gods, rang as Rama and Ravana rained blow after blow upon the head of their opponent. The bow of Rama sang as he sped arrow after arrow in the heads of Ravana, and the sword of Ravana clanged as it sought the heart of Rama. But no matter how many arrows Rama fired, the heads of Ravana regrew and multiplied, and he fought on.

"Great Prince," said Hanuman, wearing with running across the battlefield. "Remember that Ravana hides the nectar of immortality in his navel and that only the shot of a man may spill it out."

Then Rama drew his mightiest arrow and fit it to his bow. With his breath, he drew in the universe and with his string he released it. The mighty arrow struck true, and the nectar of immortality spilled from the navel of Ravana. He fell with a cry, and his fall shook the whole earth.

Thus, Rama defeated Ravana, the demon king of the Rakshasas.

Chapter 20: Sita's Purity

After the downfall of Ravana, the army of Rama celebrated. The monkeys leaped in the air, and the bears chanted, "Victory to Sri Rama! Victory to Sita, the wife of Sri Rama, released from captivity!"

Then Rama remembered the captivity of Sita and the lust of Ravana, and his heart grew cold. The words of Ravana echoed in his mind, and his heart grew colder still.

"Bring Sita to me," he said to Hanuman, and the monkey was surprised by his tone. "Let her come to me on foot."

Then Vibhishana led Sita from the city. She was worn and thin from sorrow, but her eyes shone with devotion. She rushed to Rama, Sita the lotus-eyed princess. But Rama looked away.

"For many months you have rested in a stranger's home, and so you are a stranger to me. I release you from your marriage vow, and free you to seek another husband."

The monkeys gasped, and the bears groaned and covered their eyes. Even Sugriva, the king thirsty for justice, kept his peace and was grieved. The eyes of Sita filled with tears.

"Oh my husband, my Rama! How could you accuse me of such things? Ravana forced his touch upon me in my abduction, and I abhorred and shunned it during the length of my captivity. Can you doubt my devotion to you?"

But Rama still looked away, and his lips drew into a line as stiff as the horizon. Then Sita's heart broke, and the tears spilled from her eyes and down her flawless cheeks.

"Lakshman," she said, forcing the grief from her throat. "Build me a pyre upon which to burn myself. If Rama will not take me as his wife, then my life is worth nothing but to be taken."

Then Lakshman looked beseechingly to Rama, his brother, pleading for Sita with his eyes. But still, Rama was silent and nodded his consent. Lakshman built the pyre and set it ablaze. The flames licked hungrily at the logs. Sita turned to the assembled bears, monkeys, and generals.

"Hear my testimony!" she cried and drew herself up. "If I am impure and unfaithful to my husband, the flames will consume me, and neither he nor I will suffer more."

"O Sita!" cried the bears, and their tears washed the bloody field.

"O Sita!" cried the monkeys, and their cries echoed from the skies.

Then Lakshman fell to his knees and wept, and Hanuman hid his face. But Rama was silent still, though his heart ached within him.

Sita jumped into the pyre, and the flames took her. Then the heart of Rama broke, and the tears spilled from his eyes. The sobs wracked his chest, and he fell to the ground in despair.

At this moments the gods descended, and Brahma himself pulled Sita from the fire. Her hair shone with luster, and her eyes sparkled with love and purity. Brahma presented her to Rama.

"Behold your wife, Lord Rama. She is pure beyond the fire's ability to consume her. Accept her to yourself without fear or apprehension. The separation is at an end."

Then Rama ran to Sita and took her in his arms, and called her his wife.

Thus was Sita tested and proved worthy beyond the power of fire.

Chapter 21: Krishna Steals Butter

Many years ago, Devaki gave birth to a baby boy and called him Krishna. To hide him from his uncle, Devaki delivered him to Yashoda, who cared for him as her son. Krishna loved Yashoda as his mother but didn't always obey her.

Once, when he had grown into a small child, Krishna stole a pat of butter. What sweetness! What goodness! His infant tongue yearned for more. He started slipping small pieces of butter onto his plate during meals and snuck into the kitchen during the day to taste his new favorite food. Shortly after that, there was no butter left in the house since Krishna had eaten it all.

Yashoda laughed and sighed in the same breath, for it was impossible to be angry with such an audacious and loving child.

"Krishna," she said, waving her finger. "It is not well to eat all of the butter, for then there is none for us to cook with. Please stay away from the butter."

But Krishna's taste for butter could not be stemmed by Yashoda's words. Soon he stole butter from all of the neighbors, as well, and eventually from everyone in Vrindavan. They knocked on Yashoda's door, and she listened to their complaints.

"Krishna ate my butter, and now I have none for my bread!" cried the baker, with his face covered in flour.

"Krishna ate my butter, and now I have none to cook my fish!" cried the angler, his elbows dripping with seawater.

"Krishna ate my butter, and now I have none for my children!" cried the mothers with downcast faces and wagging fingers.

Yashoda sighed, for she was tired of Krishna's naughty butter habit. She proposed a clever solution.

"To keep the butter from Krishna, tie it high up in a pitcher beyond where he can reach. Then the butter will be safe, and Krishna will not be able to steal it."

The people of Vrindavan heeded Yashoda and hung the pitchers high in their kitchens. Soon Krishna had no source of butter to quench his sweet tooth and was very put out.

One day, Yashoda left home to run an errand.

"Play safely until I return," she said, "and I shall give you a treat."

As soon as she was gone, naughty Krishna gathered all of his little friends. He pointed to the pitcher high above their heads.

"There, high above us, is a pitcher of butter. If we work together, then we can get the butter and enjoy the treat together. There is no need to wait until Yashoda returns."

The friends of Krishna clapped their hands and agreed to help him. They formed a bridge with their little arms and legs, and Krishna used them as a ladder to climb up to the butter. Ah, the golden goodness! Ah, the sweetest treat! The children enjoyed it very much, licking each spoonful clean and then dipping again for another. Laughing over their victory, they didn't hear Yashoda return. She saw the children with the butter pitcher and dirty spoons and clapped her hands to her head.

"Krishna!" she cried. "You have disobeyed me and led your friends to mischief. You shall be punished."

Then the friends of Krishna deserted him and ran from the kitchen, dropping their dirty spoons and guilty consciences by the way. Then Yashoda took Krishna and spanked him, to punish him for stealing the butter and for leading his friends astray.

Thus Lord Krishna learned the hard way to obey his elders and to honor his friends.

Chapter 22: Krishna Trades for Jewels

On another occasion, Krishna sat playing on the doorstep while his mother completed the chores. A woman passed by their home, selling delicious, plump fruit.

"Camachile, Carambola, Buddha's Hand—delicious fruits for sale," she cried.

Little Krishna looked longingly at her basket. He saw mellow langsat and imagined their bittersweet flavor. He saw purple mangosteen and sweet persimmons and yearned for the piquant ambarella.

"Ah," he thought, "If only I could taste the pink karonda or the glossy bilimbi. My mouth waters for a taste."

Krishna grabbed a handful of grains with which to trade and sprinted joyfully into the street. But the grains slipped from his little fingers as he ran, and when he arrived at the fruit basket, all of his grains were gone. Then little Krishna's eyes filled with tears and his lip trembled, for he had nothing wherewith to trade for the fruit. The fruit woman saw his sorrow and took his little hand in hers.

"Precious child!" she said. "You may take as many fruits as you like. Here, see the ripe targola. They will fit perfectly in your grip."

"But I have nothing with which to buy the fruits," said Krishna sadly, showing his empty palms. But the woman smiled.

"Whatever you have in your hands is enough for me. I accept your offering and bid you take what you like."

Then the kind fruit woman gave Krishna whatever fruits his heart desired, and he rejoiced over the dark phalsa berries and the golden mimusops. He thanked her and hugged her around the neck before skipping back to his front porch. She smiled and continued on her way.

She hadn't gone far, however, before she reached into her basket for some more fruit and bumped her fingers on hard stones. In amazement, she reached into her basket and drew forth rubies, emeralds, diamonds, and pearls. The woman gasped and dug further into the basket, which filled further with sapphires set in silver and jade set in gold.

The woman dropped to her knees and offered reverence to Vishnu for sending her a mighty gift. All the while Krishna smiled, enjoying his fruit on the doorstep.

Thus was the fruit woman rewarded for her kindness to Krishna and her devotion to Vishnu.

Chapter 23: Krishna Swallows the Flames

When Krishna grew older, his mother trusted him to tend their cows in the jungle. He and his friends drove their herds deep into the trees and undergrowth, and then played games while the cows ate their fill.

Krishna and his friends played Vish Amrit and Langdi, but Lagori, the game of stacked stones, was their favorite. Krishna stacked the rocks in a pile and then gave the ball to his friends. They threw it, knocking over the stones. Krishna rushed to the pile, stacking them up again while they tried to hit him with the ball. He was too quick, and soon all of them were laughing together.

Meanwhile, at the edge of the forest, a farmer fell asleep over his cook fire. The fire crept away and spread to the trees, consuming all in its path. Krishna's friends did not see the fire creeping behind them.

"Hit him again," they cried. "Knock out the rocks!"

Finally, the smoke drifted over them, and the cows stampeded in fear. Krishna's friends fell on their faces and wailed.

"Fire is come!" they cried. "Save us, Krishna! Save us!"

Then Krishna looked up from the game for the first time and saw the flames licking, his friends wailing, and the cows stampeding. He answered his friends calmly.

"Close your eyes," he commanded. "And I will save you."

"What?" said his friends. "What do you mean?"

"Close your eyes and do not open them again until I give you leave," said Krishna.

Then the friends of Krishna closed their eyes and put their hands over their faces, whimpering. Krishna drew in a breath as deep as the sea and swallowed all the fire. He swallowed the fire dancing in the trees. He swallowed the fire sneaking through the grasses. He swallowed the fire terrorizing the cows. When every snippet of the fire was gone, Krishna bid his friends open their eyes.

"Arise," he said. "Open your eyes."

His friends arose and peered around the clearing. The fire was gone, and the cows were saved. Even the smell of smoke was stolen from the breeze.

"Glory to Vishnu!" they cried. "Honor to Krishna and his mighty breath!"

Then Krishna and his friends gathered their cows and returned safely to their homes.

Thus Krishna preserved his friends and swallowed the fire that endangered them.

Chapter 24: Agni Spreads a Curse

Sage Bhrigu cursed Agni on behalf of his wife. In terror, Agni fled and concealed himself from God and man. Soon, the gods sent out a search party to find him. Agni jumped into the ocean and hid beneath the waves.

"They will never find me here," he thought. "The waves are too deep, and even my flames are quenched here."

But his fire burned hotter than he imagined, and soon the fish fled and the whales toned their displeasure. The frogs went to the gods and requested their aid.

"Remove Agni from the ocean, for he boils us with his heat."

The gods came to remove Agni, but he fled, cursing the frogs as he went.

"Because you have revealed me, you shall lose your sense of taste," he said. "Let that teach your tongues to wag."

Then Agni escaped the gods and took refuge in a banyan tree. The deep canopy shielded him from the sky, and the twisted roots and trailing branches hid him from view.

"Ah," thought Agni. "They won't possibly find me here. The branches are too close, and the roots reach too deep."

But a passing elephant reached into the banyan tree for his food and burned his trunk.

"Ouch!" he cried. "This banyan tree is burning!"

Then the elephant went to the gods and told them the story of the banyan tree and his burnt trunk.

"Remove Agni from the banyan tree," said the elephant, "for he burns me and I will starve."

The gods came to remove Agni, but he fled, cursing the elephant as he went.

"Because you have revealed me, you shall have a short tongue. Let that teach you to tell tales that aren't your own."

Then Agni perched in a shami tree, thinking that perhaps his flames could resemble the blushing flower pods and keep him hidden. But a colorful pitta saw him there and thought he was stealing her favorite resting place.

"Agni perches in the shami tree," she chirped. "Agni steals my favorite perch."

Then the pitta flitted to the gods and told them where Agni was hiding.

"Remove Agni from the shami tree," she asked, "for I am weary and need a place to rest."

The gods came to remove Agni, but he fled, cursing the pitta as he went.

"Because you have revealed me, you shall have a tongue that is cursed on the inside," he said. "Let that teach you to wag it too much."

Then the frogs, the elephant, and the pitta were grieved at the curses and made a ruckus in the land. The gods listened to their concerns and blessed them, each according to their worries.

The frogs, though they could no longer taste their way as did the snake, would be able to move gracefully even in darkness.

The elephant, though his tongue was short, could eat anything he wanted and lose his fear of starving to death.

The pitta, though her tongue was curved inside, could sing and warble to her heart's content. This gift of song spread to the other birds, who never forgot the curses of Agni and the gifts of the gods.

Thus Agni was found out by the animals and spread this discomfort among them.

Chapter 25: Vayu Humbles the Silk Cotton Tree

The mountains of the Himalayas stretch to the sky, a reminder of man's ascension to the Trimurti. On the slopes of these mountains grew the silk cotton tree, and its blossoms blessed the horizon. Year after year it grew larger, spreading its branches even further into the sky. Then the tree was happy in fulfilling its purpose and provided blossoms for all who passed by.

One day Narada, the storyteller, passed by with his khartal jingling. He sat beneath the silk cotton tree to rest and to play his instruments. The drone of his tambura pleased the tree, and it stood very still to hear each note and swell.

"How beautifully you play," said the tree. "Truly you are the master of Mahathi."

Narada smiled and bowed.

"Thank you. I have worked many years to master its ways."

Then the tree fell silent, wondering if it, too, could master something and earn glory in the world, as did Narada. It could not travel to the lokas, the hidden realms, but surely it could master its own gentle slope. In the meantime Narada rested his head at its roots and admired the tree, looking up into its steady branches.

"How great you have grown, silk cotton tree," he said. "Your branches that stretch toward the heavens are firm and strong. Not even a mighty storm could shake them."

"Ah," said the tree, thinking quickly. "I grow strong and firm because the storm is my servant. It knows better than to blow on its master."

Narada raised his eyebrows but said nothing. He thanked the tree for its shade and continued on his way. Later, he met Vayu, the god of wind and storms.

"Hello, Vayu!" he said. "I know you love a good story. You'll never believe what I heard the silk cotton tree say."

"Tell me, Narada," laughed Vayu, "for your stories are more entertaining than leaves dancing in a breeze."

Then Narada told Vayu what the silk cotton tree had said—that it was the master of the storm and therefore kept its leaves always because the wind could not shake its branches. Then the face of Vayu turned dour.

"What, does the silk cotton tree think itself so powerful?" he asked. "I'll show it in a moment where the truth lies."

Then Vayu flew to the Himalayas and confronted the tree, tousling its leaves with his breath.

"Hear, silk cotton tree. You are not the master of the storm. You spoke to bluster, but the breezes do not heed your command."

The proud tree refused to acknowledge its mistake and ignored Vayu. This only angered Vayu further. He blustered through the tree's branches.

"Listen, silk cotton tree. I do not blow on you out of respect for Brahma. When he created the world, he stopped to rest on one of your branches. It is his holiness and not your mastery that I honor."

Still, the tree kept its peace. Vayu's face darkened, and he worked himself into a great storm. The winds tore at the hillside and stripped the silk cotton tree of its blushing leaves and blossoms. The tree sighed over the leaves littering its roots, but could not return them to their places.

Thus the tree was punished for its arrogance and lost its leaves like every other.

Chapter 26: Savitri Chooses a Husband

Once, in the Madra Kingdom, there lived a king who longed for a child. He and his consort, Malavi, prayed and prayed for an heir to continue their line. At last, they were sent a daughter, and they named her Savitri.

Savitri grew up beautiful and pure. Her hair flowed like the river Ganges, and her lotus eyes smiled on all she saw. In fact, when the time came for her to marry, none sought her hand; she was too beautiful, too pure for any suitor in her land. Her father called her to him.

"My daughter," said King Ashwapati, "since none here seek your hand, you must seek your own husband. Find the son of a king for my sake, and for your own seek a man of noble heart."

"Thank you, my father," Savitri replied. "I will travel and search out a husband the best I may."

Then Savitri left her father's palace. She left behind her gold, her jewels, and her fine silk saris and took up a hermit's pack, replete with the necessary materials for her journey. She walked many miles, seeking a husband to meet her father's qualifications. After many days of travel, she came across a blind man in a forest, scratching near the roots of trees for food.

"Here, good hermit," she said, offering him some fruit. "Take some food from my pack that I may not be grieved by your hunger."

The hermit nodded gratefully and accepted the meal.

"And from what fair voice and hand do I receive so ample a gift?" he asked, as he devoured the meal.

"I am Savitri," she replied, "daughter of Ashwapati and Malavi."

"The princess?" said the blind man. "Ah, that I am blind! I had heard you described as a great beauty of open heart and mind. Could you describe yourself for me?"

Savitri tried, but couldn't give the hermit a clear description of herself. He smiled and called his son, Satyavan.

"My son," said the hermit. "Can you describe for me the Princess Savitri?"

Then Satyavan looked on the princess, and his heart yearned for hers in an instant. But he restrained himself and said instead, "Oh my father, she is as beautiful as the sun rising. Her eyes shine like the stars in the night sky, and her face is open to the tune of Dharma. Her hair flows like the sacred river, and the curve of her lips speaks peace and truth."

Then the heart of Savitri quivered in her, and she looked favorably on Satyavan.

"Oh," she thought, "that I could gratify my father as well as myself. Satyavan's heart knows the way of Dharma and his soul is open to truth."

Then Savitri sighed, and made to bid the hermit goodbye.

"Thank you for your conversation," she said, glancing at Satyavan, "but I must continue on my mission."

"Your mission?" asked the hermit. "What is that? And may we help?"

Then the heart of Savitri ached for Satyavan even more, and she sighed again.

"I seek a husband noble both in birth and in heart, for none have courage to woo me in my own country."

"Princess," said the hermit, bowing deeply. "Look favorably on my son, Satyavan. He is noble in both birth and in heart, for I am the King Dyumatsena of the Kingdom of Salwa. My eyesight and kingdom were taken from me, and I am left a hermit here in the forest. Bless my son, Satyavan, and consent to be his wife."

Then Princess Savitri smiled, and the brightness of her joy rivaled the light of the sun. King Dyumatsena placed her hand in the hand of Satyavan, and her heart knit with his.

Thus was Princess Savitri promised to Satyavan, son of King Dyumatsena.

Chapter 27: Savitri's Fidelity

When Savitri returned to her father's court, she found the shades of mourning hanging near the door and Narada, the storyteller and messenger of Vishnu, in audience.

She bowed deeply to her father and Narada and joyfully told them about her choice to marry Satyavan. Then Narada's face grew grave, and he rested his tambura upon the ground.

"Princess," he said. "You have made a poor decision. Satyavan is indeed noble both in birth and in heart, but his destiny is already writ before him. A year from today he will die, and you will be left husbandless as you were before."

"My daughter!" said King Ashwapati. "Please, choose another and spare yourself this aggravation."

But Princess Saravati drew herself up.

"I will choose a husband but once, and I have chosen Satyavan."

"So be it," said Narada, and he nodded approvingly. King Ashwapati was grieved, but granted the wish of Savitri. She and Satyavan made saptapadi, their vows in the presence of sacred fire, and their marriage began in peace. Savitri left behind the wealth of her childhood and donned the guise of a hermit, and lived happily with Satyavan in the forest.

A year passed. Each day seemed like a blink to Savitri, so deep was her love for her husband. Then finally arrived the day when Satyavan was predicted to die. Savitri asked permission to accompany him into the forest, and they entered with heavy hearts.

"Though I am to die," said Satyavan, picking up his axe, "I would leave you with enough wood to keep our home warm."

Savitri kissed his hand and bid him work. After a time, the face of Satyavan grew pale and strained, and he placed his head in Savitri's lap. She watered him with her tears as her heart choked within her breast.

Out of the trees came Yama himself, the god of the dead, sent to fetch the soul of Satyavan. Yama stripped the soul of Satyavan away and turned back into the forest, and the trees bent back to offer him passage. Savitri followed sadly, tracing the steps of Yama and following the soul of Satyavan. After a time, Yama noticed Savitri behind him.

"Princess," he said. "Turn back and take another husband, for the destiny of Satyavan is to die today."

"I cannot turn back," said Savitri. "I am obedient to Dharma, which dictates fidelity and obedience and friendship with the strict. I am not afraid to follow the path of a just ruler such as yourself, the King of Dharma. From you, I can expect the truth, nobility of mind and conduct."

Yama was surprised to hear such wisdom but still attempted to dissuade her.

"The path is not for you," he said. "It is the destiny of Satyavan to die today."

"I will not turn back," said Savitri, and repeated her words as they were before.

"Take any boon, then," said Yama, and added quickly, "save that of Satyavan's life."

"I have but three wishes, great Yama," said Savitri. "First, restore the sight and kingdom of Dyumatsena, for he lives in accordance with Dharma. Second, grant him a hundred children for my father, to carry on the name of his line. Third, grant me and my husband, Satyavan, a hundred children, that I may be compensated for his loss."

Then Yama was trapped, for how could he grant this boon without returning the life of Satyavan?

"Very well," he said. "This boon, since you asked in wisdom and fidelity, shall be granted."

Then Yama returned Satyavan's soul and honored Savitri for her courage and dedication. When Satyavan awoke, Savitri cradled him in her arms, crying, and told him the whole story. Their tears mingled, and they offered tapasya to both Brahma and Vishnu.

Thus Savitri saved her husband through fidelity and wisdom and petitioned Yama, the god of the dead.

Chapter 28: Chitragupta Takes Notes

Lord Brahma, the creator, went one day to visit Yama, the god of the dead. Lord Brahma passed the hounds that guarded the road, and their heads bowed to do him homage. He passed the buffalo, tethered in its pasture, upon which Yama rode through the earth. At length, he passed a line of waiting souls.

"What are you waiting for, souls of men?" asked Lord Brahma.

"For the judgment of Yama," they answered.

Lord Brahma continued down the line. He passed more souls, tall and short, lanky and robust.

"What are you waiting for, souls of men?" he asked.

"For the judgment of Yama," they answered.

Lord Brahma walked faster and faster until he reached the judgment seat of Yama.

"Good day, Yama," he said. "I have come to pay you a visit."

"To Swas," said Yama, with a bow.

"What?" said Lord Brahma, surprised. Yama shook his head.

"Not you. The souls. I send them to the swarga, the heaven, they need. There is no one else to judge and assign them."

"To Swas," said Yama again, and a soul passed onto the path that would take it to the realm of Indra.

Lord Brahma looked at the line of human souls awaiting judgment; it stretched out of his sight. Yama greeted the next soul and began the review of the soul's doings, good and bad. Yama reviewed the soul's actions, the reverences it made, and the tapasyas it performed. He reviewed its thoughts, its goings and comings, and doings of every day of its life. Finally, the review was finished.

"To Tharus," said Yama, and turned to the next soul. Lord Brahma saw the lines on Yama's brow and heard the shuffle of the souls waiting to receive judgment.

"Yama, is there no other way to judge the dead?" he asked.

"I was the first mortal who died, and thus assumed the burden of rule of the dead," said Yama. "Who else might assist me in my work?"

Lord Brahma thought, and from his thought sprung Chitragupta. Immediately Chitragupta took out his pen and a leaf and began to write more quickly than a gazelle in the field.

"Farmer, yes. Good father, yes. Did not honor Shiva, no. Offended a Rishi, no. Recommended for Bhuvas."

"Agreed," said Yama, and the soul started on its path. With Chitragupta's help, the line sped more quickly. Chitragupta studied the lives of men, recording their doings with his pen and leaf. When the time came to recommend them to one of the swargas or to return them to Bhoomi, the earth, Chitragupta had the summaries of each soul ready. He knew whether to send them deeper into Naraka to expiate sins or to send them to Maha, the swarga governed by Brahma himself. He knew the gateway to Thaarus and the formula for a good life and etched them on his records. Then Yama was pleased and thanked Lord Brahma for his help.

Thus became Chitragupta, who summarizes the lives of mortal men and recommends them for heaven.

Chapter 29: Ashes to Ashes

Bhasmasura sought a boon from Shiva. He performed tapasya and waited on Parvati for many years. He fasted and subjected himself to the elements. At last Lord Shiva heard his prayers.

"What boon do you seek from me, Bhasmasura?" he asked.

"Oh great Lord," Bhasmasura answered. "I wish to be as the ashes that cover your sacred flesh. Grant that whomever I touch on the head with my hands shall burn to ashes, that all might become sacred as you are."

"Let it be done," said Shiva. Then the eyes of Bhasmasura glinted with guile.

"Then come, great Lord," he said, "and turn to ashes yourself. For only when you are gone may I possess your wife, Parvati, and worship her as forcefully as I have desired."

Then Bhasmasura pursued Shiva, trying to touch him with his hands. Shiva raced through the forests and across the deserts, but Bhasmasura pursued him still. Finally, Shiva fell before Vishnu and begged his help.

"The demon Bhasmasura seeks my life and my wife," Shiva cried. "He uses my boon against me, and I will be turned to ashes."

Vishnu changed his form to Mohini, the beautiful enchantress. He danced in the path of Bhasmasura, drawing the demon's attention from Shiva.

"Marry me, Mohini," said Bhasmasura, mesmerized by her dance. "My heart and hand yearn after you."

"I will marry none but him who loves to dance as much as I," said Mohini, laughing. "Can you mimic my movements and prove yourself a proper husband?"

Bhasmasura, blinded by desire, agreed. When Mohini twirled, so did he. He followed her bharatanatyam and swayed through the symbols of odissi. They danced for many days until Bhasmasura lost suspicion and thought only of the beautiful Mohini and gaining her as his wife. At last, Mohini twirled to finish, placing her hand on her head. After dancing for so long, Bhasmasura forgot Shiva's boon and placed his hand on his head.

Poof! Bhasmasura turned to ashes.

Thus Shiva was saved by the interference of Vishnu and learned to be more wary of his gifts.

Preview of Roman Mythology
A Captivating Guide to Roman Gods, Goddesses, and Mythological Creatures

Introduction

Gravitas was a founding principle of Roman society. Life can be brutal, and the Romans figured out early that guiding one's actions with weightiness or seriousness—or, in today's word—intentionality—was necessary. Using *gravitas* as a guide for life made them exceptionally practical—although not particularly creative. In fact, the Romans were an unimaginative society. The creativity they did employ was greatly borrowed –sometimes forcibly--from other cultures.

Only a few of their gods were entirely Roman. Because little is written during the early years of Rome, it is difficult to separate their own divinities as opposed to those they appropriated.

Originally, the Romans were farmers. Many of their earliest gods dealt with crops, rain, and their main river—the Tiber.

Gravitas, with its intentionality and practicality, led the Romans to think affinities could be cultivated by making their gods look like those of their neighbors. These affinities made assimilation or conquest much easier. Allowing citizens to keep their religious traditions, a widespread practice among some early civilizations, helped make them more compliant with Roman rule. And if Roman traditions looked like the traditions of the conquered peoples, the subjugated populace would believe they truly belonged to Rome.

Like a modern exercise in building a commercial brand, Roman writers of the first century BC developed stories of Roman myth and history to manufacture legitimacy for their rulers. Virgil (70–19 BC), for instance, gave Rome its most important work of authority—the *Aeneid*, which told the story of Rome's roots in the Trojan War; they were descended from Trojans, the enemies of the Greeks. We'll take a brief look at the truth of this possibility in "Chapter 4 — Borrowings from Etruria."

The Shape of Things to Come

We will look at many aspects of the Roman gods, goddesses, and mythological creatures. Each of the first six chapters begins with a narrative scene which helps bring the legendary and mythical characters to life.

In chapter 1, we explore the seeds of legitimacy that Virgil planted regarding the Trojan connection to Rome. Though Aeneas was a minor character in Homer's epic *Iliad*, Virgil shows Aeneas to be the epitome of what a good Roman should be—heroic, serious, virtuous, and devoted. And, important to the *Iliad*, Aeneas was one of the sons of Venus or, as she was known to the Greeks, Aphrodite—the goddess of love.

How do we get from a Trojan demigod to the reality of Rome? This is the topic of chapter 2. In this chapter, we explore the foundation of that great city by the semi-divine, wolf-suckled brothers, Romulus and Remus. We also consider the myth of Aeneas's son, Ascanius, who was also known as Iulus—the basis of the name of Julius, and the basis of the Julio-Claudian dynasty of the Roman Empire. Virgil gave the family of Julius Caesar its back-story to make his patron, and Rome's first emperor, Augustus, seem worthier of being a living god.

In chapter 3, we examine the gods of Roman origin as well as Roman mythological creatures.

Chapter 4 focuses on the Etruscan influence on Roman mythology. Latin culture co-opted Minerva as its own, and then gave her the Greek attributes of the goddess Athena.

Perhaps the strongest influence in Roman mythology came from the Greeks. The Greeks were far more creative, and their legends were far richer and more detailed. The Greek influence is the topic of chapter 5. The Greeks had expanded their influence to the southern portion of the Italian peninsula far from the tiny Kingdom of Rome. In the centuries before the Roman Republic, the Greeks had expanded into southern France and eastern Spain.

In chapter 6, we delve into the world of Celtic influence and see how the gods of the Celts were melded with the Roman pantheon in creative ways. What we know about the Celtic pantheon comes from the Romans. The Celts used oral storytelling to record their history for generations.

Finally, in chapter 7, we take a brief look at the potential truths behind the Roman gods, goddesses, and creatures. Every myth had a beginning, and in this chapter, we explore some of the possibilities.

The Romans were builders and innovators in many industries. They took existing resources and shaped them to suit their needs. But they also adopted the creative ideas of others. Over time, the Roman pantheon became increasingly a melting pot of ideas blended into a cultural potpourri.

Chapter 1 — The Trojan Connection

Goddess Juno—Jupiter's queen—looked down upon the ragtag fleet of Trojan ships, led by Aeneas, and she sneered with delight as she thought of sinking them to the bottom of the sea. Juno despised Troy and its people. Petty and immature, like all the gods and goddesses—they lacked the maturity and humility to act wisely.

She hated Troy because of Paris, Prince of Troy, snubbed Juno when he judged who was the most beautiful goddess—between Juno (the Greek Hera), Minerva (Athena) and Venus (Aphrodite).

The dispute began at the wedding of the Greek goddess, Thetis, to King Peleus of Aegina.

One goddess, though, despised the event. Eris, goddess of discord, and daughter of Jupiter and Juno was not being invited because the other gods wanted a peaceful event. Her exclusion angered her. She said, "to the fairest one" and threw a golden apple over the wall and into the party. No one caught the apple, but three goddesses claimed the golden apple as her own—Juno, Minerva, and Venus. To settle the dispute, they asked Jupiter to judge between them.

Understanding the potentially dire consequences of such a task, Jupiter chose a mortal to judge who should own the apple based on the inscription: "to the fairest one." That mortal was the fair-minded Paris, Prince of Troy. Jupiter understandably protected himself by choosing Paris, since the choice would upset the two goddesses not selected—and that hostility might last forever. Jupiter protected his own sanity and safety by transferring the dangerous duty onto an expendable and convenient mortal. Perhaps even wise Minerva did not realize how truly foolish Paris would be to accept such an inherently dangerous task.

After the wedding celebration was over Mercury (Hermes) escorted the three goddesses to Asia Minor—also known as Anatolia, or modern Turkey. There, they bathed in a local spring on Mount Ida, not very far from Troy. After freshening up, they found Paris, sitting on a log under the shade of a mature tree, tending to his flock on the slopes of the mountain. Naturally, the prince was surprised to have the three lovely goddesses present him with this interesting challenge.

At first, the goddesses posed before the honest prince--Juno, Minerva and finally Venus. But Paris could not decide.

"I'm afraid, my ladies," he said, taking a deep breath before continuing, "that this is an impossible task. You are each incredibly beautiful, and my mind is at an impasse."

"What if we were to show you our full form," asked Venus, "without the visual impediment of the divine clothing we typically wear out of sensible modesty?"

The other two goddesses nodded encouragingly.

Paris smiled. He had seen naked women before and knew the pleasure that came with the sight. In fact, his wife was the beautiful mountain nymph, Oenone. The thought that three major goddesses would willingly bare themselves for his judgment aroused him more than he thought possible.

He spoke cautiously, though. He knew of their power, and he did not want to answer rashly and risk offending any of them.

"I can sense the importance of this challenge you've given me. If it pleases each of you that I—a mere mortal—view your beauty in its entirety to complete the charge you've laid upon me, then I will humbly do this thing as you request. I sincerely hope that this will be enough to settle in my own mind an answer to your question."

Again, Juno went first because of her seniority amongst the three goddesses. Quietly, she unfastened her garment and let it fall to her feet. Slowly, she stepped out of it and moved toward the young man as he remained seated.

Closer she came, slowly advancing. When she was close enough to touch, she showed the young man her neck and breasts down to her abdomen. She showed him her thighs and buttocks, as well as the small of her back. As she displayed her physical form in all its splendor, she whispered to him, bribing him in exchange for his vote for her. She would give him rule over all of Europe and Asia, and not merely Asia Minor—from Eriu to Yamato—Ireland to Japan.

As Juno returned to her clothes, the other two goddesses guessed what she had done. Each secretly decided to sway the young prince's decision with the best possible bribe they could consider.

Next, Minerva dropped her clothing and approached Paris, equally seductively. Because of her temperament as a warrior and protectress of the homeland, her movements added power and finesse which Juno lacked. Her earthiness left Paris breathless. As Minerva displayed up-close each curve of her beautiful body, she whispered to him that she could make the young prince the wisest and most skilled of all mortals in the art of war. All he would need to do was to choose her as the owner of the golden apple.

Moments later, as Minerva restored her vestments, Venus dropped her gown and stepped forward, turning with a coy seduction that left the young mortal's heart pounding with each step. This was the goddess of love and Paris felt once again the impossibility of this challenge.

Venus promised that if Paris chose her, she would make it possible for him to marry the most beautiful mortal woman in all the world—the already married, Helen, wife of King Menelaus of Sparta.

Assailed by so much feminine charm, the bribe which raked most heavily across his mind was the one that most closely matched the feelings overpowering his mind, body, and soul. Helplessly, he chose Venus and thus sealed the fate of Troy, setting in motion events that would eventually lead to the creation of Rome.

When Helen left her husband to join Paris in Troy, the Greeks banded together to attack the Trojan capital. Why would there be such unity amongst the usually conflicting Greek city-states? The leaders of those city-states had agreed to that attack.

Helen was so beautiful that almost every king in the Greek kingdoms sought her hand in marriage. Her wise father feared any man he chose for his daughter would soon lose her because the others would continue to fight over her, even after she married. Minerva's wisdom guided him to bind each king to the father's decision by swearing to protect Helen's marriage to whomever she was to be pledged. Only after each king gave his pledge did the father reveal his choice.

Thus, when Helen left her husband, the other Greek kings were duty-bound to go after her—to protect her marriage to Menelaus of Sparta. For a decade, they laid siege to Troy to protect those wedding vows between Menelaus and Helen. In the end, Troy lost, and the city was destroyed.

Now that Juno and Minerva had ensured the collapse of Troy, after its ten-year war against the Greeks, its remaining citizens were dispersed throughout the eastern Mediterranean. The future heritage of Troy depended upon Aeneas, second cousin of the now dead princes of Troy—including Hector, Paris, Deiphobus, Polydorus.

Juno despised Troy for several reasons.

From her great height, Juno also looked down upon her favorite city—Carthage—and dreaded the thought the descendants of Aeneas would someday ruin the now-fledgling town. If only she could stop Aeneas and end the prophecy concerning him.

Juno also despised the Trojans because her own daughter, Hebe, had been replaced as Jupiter's cupbearer. Her husband had chosen instead the Trojan, Catamitus (Greek Ganymede).

After the destruction of Troy, Aeneas had directed his ships to head west. Somewhere out there was a new home for him and his people.

Slowly, at first, and then with conviction, Juno descended down to Earth and to the island of Aeolus—master of the winds.

"My dear King Aeolus," said Juno.

"My goddess!" Aeolus stood back, amazed at her sudden entrance. "To what do I owe this honor."

Juno looked away for a moment, considering her words carefully, then turned back to him with a look that drilled into his eyes, commanding his full attention, even though she already had it. "I have come to ask a favor. A tiny thing, really. It's trivial, but it needs to be done."

"Yes, my lady?"

"I would like you to use your winds to create a storm. Over there," she pointed out to sea, "are the ships of Aeneas, the Trojan prince, and all his fellow refugees. I want them destroyed—especially the ship holding Aeneas."

"Hmm-mm," Aeolus nodded thoughtfully, then shook his head in disagreement. "My lady, I cannot. I have no grievance with Aeneas or his people."

"But you must," said Juno. "Perhaps I could make the task more attractive by including Deiopea to become your bride."

The king's eyebrows raised in appreciation of the offer. The sea nymph, Deiopea, was said to be the loveliest of all sea creatures. But he shook his head again. "My lady, I will not take her as wife, for I already have one, and she is sufficient for me. But because this means so much to you, I will help."

"Thank you, kind sir," said Juno, and abruptly vanished.

Immediately, Aeolus gathered all his winds and overwhelmed the Trojan fleet. This storm disturbed the surface of the sea, and suddenly, Neptune (Greek Poseidon) was alerted to the commotion in his realm.

"What goes on here?" Neptune demanded. He saw the winds and their target—the Trojan ships. The sea god had no love for Troy, but he resented the intrusion into his domain. "Be still, waters!" he commanded. And he calmed the winds, despite the efforts of Aeolus. This was Neptune's territory, and any intrusion by another god was unwelcome.

Neptune could smell the handiwork of Aeolus and knew someone else was behind this attack. Despite his dislike of the Trojans, he disliked the intrusion even more. So, he gave the ships of Aeneas a favorable breeze which took them to the north coast of Africa, not far from the new town of Carthage.

Aeneas and his fellow travelers landed on the shore, thankful to be alive.

In the distance, Aeneas saw a beautiful woman approaching on horseback. She had a bow strung across her shoulder and a quiver on her back. He watched her as she made her way to them.

"You are all lucky to be alive," said the woman, who happened to be his mother, Venus, in disguise. "Some of the gods favor you and your companions."

"I was beginning to lose hope," said Acneas. "I appreciate your words, but even I was beginning to wonder if all of the gods might be against us, now that we have lost our war with the Greeks."

"Fear not," she said, "your destiny is to plant the seed of a great empire."

The young prince cocked his head to the side, uncertain he could believe this from some strange huntress on the beach of North Africa.

"And you are in luck," she said. "Not far this way," she pointed toward the West, "there is a new town called Carthage, founded by the Phoenicians of Tyre, and ruled over by good queen Dido. You will usually find her in the Temple of Juno."

"Well, thank you, fair stranger," said Aeneas, just as she prodded her horse into a trot in the same direction. "But—" and she was gone, receding into the distance, ignoring his words.

"I see trees over there, master," said one of his fellow travelers. "There may be a well and clean water."

"Good. Let's us refresh ourselves and then head toward this new town, Carthage."

Aeneas found his way to the Temple of Juno and there entreated the queen to help his small band of refugees. In the tradition of all civilized folk, she invited him and his fellow travelers to a banquet in their honor.

In the meantime, Venus met with her son, Cupid—half-brother to Aeneas.

"My darling son, I need your help. I would like you to help me create a bond between Queen Dido and your brother, Aeneas."

"Yes, mother."

At the banquet which Dido arranged for Aeneas and the other Trojans, Cupid showed up disguised as Ascanius, Aeneas's son by his first wife, Creusa. While the image of the son approached Queen Dido bearing gifts, invisible Venus surrounded the real Ascanius with a ghostly shroud to keep others from noticing there were two of him. Even the real Ascanius was bewitched into ignoring the imposter.

Dido graciously received the gifts and reached for the handsome young boy to draw him close. She felt an overpowering urge to give him a mother's affection. While in Dido's embrace, Cupid worked his charms on her, weakening a sacred pledge she had made to stay faithful to her dead husband, slain by her brother.

"Tell me, Aeneas," said Queen Dido, "all that has happened to you. I want to hear the entire story. Stories help us to understand." She was going to say that stories also entertain, but thought better of it, knowing the Trojan's tale would include great tragedy.

"Well, my lady," said Aeneas, "I would like to thank you for your gracious hospitality. We are weary from our travels. This spot of civilization soothes our souls."

The queen raised her cup toward him and smiled.

"Our once-great city," said Aeneas, "at the entrance to that enormous body of water, northeast of the Mediterranean—what the Greeks call the Euxine Sea—our city was attacked by the Greeks. For ten long years, they tried to destroy us all. Then, on the eve of what seemed like our victory, the Greeks left a gift on our doorstep and departed en masse. But the gift was our undoing, for within it was Greek soldiers who lay as still as death until we were drunk and asleep from our long celebration.

"By the end of the next day, our city was a smoldering mass of former humanity. Our people killed or under Greek subjugation. Some of us escaped inland. The next day, when the hostilities were done, and some semblance of peace returned, I went back to Troy to find my wife, but she was dead. In the smoke, I saw an image of her, and it spoke, telling me I would establish a great city to the West.

"Inspired by her words, I convinced my fellows to help me build our small fleet of ships. Our travels took us all over the Eastern Mediterranean—to Thrace, where we found the remains of our fellow Trojan, Polydorus. Then to Strophades, where we met Celaeno, the Harpy. She told us to leave her island. And before we left, she said I must look for a place called Italy. After that, we landed at Crete. We thought perhaps we arrived at our destination and began to build our city. We named it Pergamea. But then Apollo visited us and told us we had not yet arrived at our true destination.

"At fair Buthrotum, north of Macedonia, we attempted to replicate Troy. On that island, we met the widow of Prince Hector and found Prince Helenus who had also escaped. Now, Helenus has the gift of prophecy. From him, I learned more about my own destiny. He told me I needed to find Italy which is also known as Ausonia, and by the name Hesperia."

"There are two large peninsulas named Hesperia," said the queen. "One is due north of here, across the Tyrrhenian Sea. The other is at the far western end of the Mediterranean, north of the exit to our small, inland sea, and entrance to a far larger, Great Ocean, the realm of Atlas and the once great Atlantis which sank so long ago."

The queen suddenly felt self-conscious about what she had just said. The Phoenician custom was to keep secret the discoveries of the Phoenician people. Such discoveries were frequently made at great cost and to give them away would be to lose the Phoenician hold on such knowledge. But the queen had been feeling exceptionally joyous with the arrival of these guests. She felt overcome with a generous spirit.

"Thank you, my lady, for your help in our quest. After Buthrotum, we found ourselves in a land called Trinacria where our ships barely escaped a grave danger we later learned was called Charybdis—a vast whirlpool which threatened to swallow entire ships. From there, we encountered the Cyclopes and one of the Greeks—a soldier who had served under Ulysses—a soldier who had been left behind in their mad rush to escape the great, one-eyed beasts. We took Achaemenides, the Greek, on board with us, but barely escaped with our own lives when blind Polyphemus heard our voices. Not long afterward, my own father, Anchises, died peacefully of his own years. We sailed next into the open seas, unsure where to find this Hesperia—this Italy. A great storm nearly destroyed us, but then we found the coast not far from here."

"I am so thankful that you made it," said the queen. Her eyes glistened toward him, and at that moment, she knew she loved this prince.

Aeneas, too, could feel the bond and gazed upon her with deep admiration.

Later, after they had taken in their fill, Dido suggested Aeneas, and a few of his best hunters go inland with her to find game.

In the hall, but invisible to these mortals, Juno confronted Venus.

"Listen," said Juno. "I would like to strike a bargain with you. These two seem to be well-suited for one another. See how much they are in love?"

"Yes," said Venus, "what did you have in mind."

"I will stop my attacks on these Trojans if Aeneas stays here in Carthage with Dido, becoming her husband."

Venus smiled at the thought of her son marrying the local queen. This pleased her greatly. And since she already orchestrated the beginnings of love, she would do everything she could to hold Juno to her promise.

During their hunt, Dido and Aeneas followed their clues to find their prey and became separated from the others. And when a storm struck they found a nearby cave for shelter. Within the cave, Aeneas held Dido close to keep her warm. In that embrace, there came kisses and a deeper, more passionate experience which Dido took to mean Aeneas was now bound to her for life.

After they returned to the palace in Carthage, the two were clearly and deeply in love. But their affection was short-lived. While the two were together in her chamber, a bright light appeared in the middle of the room and suddenly there appeared the form of Mercury, messenger of the gods.

"Aeneas, son of Venus," said Mercury, "this has gone too far, and Jupiter himself has commanded me to intervene. You have a destiny, and it must be seen through to the end."

"But," said Dido. "does he have to stay away. Can't he return to me?"

"I'm afraid not, my lady," replied Mercury. "The future fate of the world hangs on the shoulders of Aeneas."

Dido shook her head and screamed in agony. The pain of such fresh love being snuffed out before its full blossom was too much to bear. She looked to Aeneas for some relief from her agony.

"Sorry, my love," was all he could say.

Her screams filled the palace with such remorse all could feel her pain.

Immediately, she grabbed the sword of Aeneas and left the room.

Cautiously, he followed. He could hear her commands to build a pyre in the great opening in front of the palace. When it had been built, she climbed up to the top of it, his sword in her hand.

"People of Carthage. We've all suffered too much tragedy of late. First, the murder of my husband, and now this tragic love that must never be. Suddenly, she plunged the sword into her abdomen.

Her eyes goggled in incredible pain, and she dropped to her knees, the sword sliding from her wound. "There will forever be great strife between our peoples, Aeneas. You have wounded me more than this sword could ever do." She then fell backward onto the pyre, gasping these final words, "rise up from my bones, avenging spirit."

Understanding the gravity of this act, Aeneas quickly gathered his people and ushered them out of the city and back to their ships.

As they sailed away, he looked back at Carthage, but all he could see was the smoke pouring upward into the sky from Dido's funeral pyre.

What History and an Analysis of Myth Tell Us

Estimates for the founding of Carthage range from 1215 to 814 BC. Modern historians seem to favor the later date, because of a reference made by Timaeus of Taormina that Carthage had been founded 38 years before the first Olympiad (776 BC). This is ironic and possibly quite wrong, if we believe the story of Aeneas, because the Trojan

War was supposedly far earlier—traditionally dated at 1184 BC. Some historians placed the founding of Gadir (Roman Gādēs, Moorish Qādis, modern Cádiz, Spain) at about 1104 BC, as a colony of Tyre—far beyond Carthage when traveling from Tyre. While it's entirely possible that Tyre bypassed many locations to establish a lonely outpost beyond the far, opposite end of the Mediterranean, it seems more likely they created at least one or two intermediate colonies across that 4,000-kilometer length. The archaeological level at Hissarlik, Turkey, associated with the Trojan War, called Troy VIIa was destroyed about 1220 BC.

Though Aeneas has minor mention in Homer's *Iliad* the myth of Aeneas being the grandfather of Rome came about during the first century with writers like Virgil, Ovid, and Livy. So, it seems highly probable the Roman connection to Troy, was contrived to establish a pseudo-historical basis for the Julian family brand.

From this fictionalized narrative, Julius Caesar could claim direct descent from the goddess Venus, through her son, the Trojan Aeneas. In addition, Aeneas's father, Anchises, was fourth grandson of Zeus and Electra. Thus, every time a member of the Caesar family spoke, they were speaking from a position of divine power, and this helped them to command greater respect. It didn't save Julius Caesar from the conspiracy to assassinate him, but it did help to lay the foundation of "gravitas" that grew into the office of emperor.

Venus was the goddess of love, but Julius Caesar had made a name for himself, and his extended family, more from his own acts of war—against the Celtic Gauls, and later against disruptive elements within the Roman Republic.

From these histories (contrived or handed down), we learn which gods favored the Romans and their founders.

Some of the other gods were no friend to Rome and its founding. These defacto enemies of Troy, and thus, by implication, of Rome, were Juno (Greek Hera), Vulcan (Hephaestus), Mercury (Hermes), Neptune (Poseidon), Thetis (no counterpart in Roman mythology), Timorus (Phobos), Formido (Deimos) and Discordia (Eris). Discordia (Eris), after all, was the goddess who had started the entire Trojan problem with her jealous spitefulness for not being invited to a divine wedding. It seems doubly abusive she should be against the party being attacked because of her own behavior. Supporting Troy, and by inference, also Rome, were Venus (Aphrodite), Apollo, Mars (Ares), Diana (Artemis), Latona (Leto) and Greek Scamander (no Roman equivalent).

From the expanded story of Aeneas, by the Romans, we see Jupiter also supported the Roman cause.

From Aeneas, the son of Venus down to the founders of Rome—Romulus and Remus—there were 15 generations of Latins, first at Lavinium and then at Alba Longa.

In the next chapter, we see how these divine, Trojan demigods struggled to establish a beachhead in the middle of the Italian peninsula, amongst numerous other tribes.

Check out this book

ROMAN MYTHOLOGY

A CAPTIVATING GUIDE TO ROMAN GODS, GODDESSES, AND MYTHOLOGICAL CREATURES

MATT CLAYTON

Bibliography

Chatterjee, Debjani. *The Elephant-Headed God and Other Hindu Tales*. Oxford University Press, 1992.

Doniger O'Flaherty, Wendy. *Hindu Myths: A Sourcebook Translated from Sanskrit*. Penguin Books, 1994.

Dowson, John. *A Classical Dictionary of Hindu Mythology and Religion, Geography, History, and Culture*. DK Printworld, 2014.

Egenes, Linda and Kumunda Reddy. *The Ramayana: A New Retelling of Valmiki's Ancient Epic—Complete and Comprehensive*. TarcherPerigree, 2016.

Mathur, Suresh Narain and B.K. Chaturvedi. *The Diamond Book of Hindu Gods and Goddesses: Their Hierarchy and Other Holy Things*. Diamond Pocket Books, 2005.

Murray, Alexander S. *The Manual of Mythology: Greek and Roman, Norse and Old German, Hindoo and Egyptian Mythology*. Newcastle Publishing, 1993.

Patel, Sanjay. *Ramayana: Divine Loophole*. Chronicle Books, 2010.

Free Bonus from Captivating History (Available for a Limited time)

Hi History Lovers!

Now you have a chance to join our exclusive history list so you can get your first history ebook for free as well as discounts and a potential to get more history books for free! Simply visit the link below to join.

Captivatinghistory.com/ebook

Also, make sure to follow us on:

Twitter: @Captivhistory

Facebook: Captivating History:@captivatinghistory

Printed in Great Britain
by Amazon